Out of Sight

Out of Sight

Scott Frank

from the novel by
Elmore Leonard

First published in 1998
by ScreenPress Books
28 Castle Street Eye Suffolk IP23 7AW

Photoset by Parker Typesetting Service, Leicester
Printed in England by Clays Ltd, St Ives plc

A CIP record for this book
is available from the British Library

ISBN 1 901680 23 1

For more information on forthcoming ScreenPress Books,
contact the publishers at:

ScreenPress Books
28 Castle Street
Eye Suffolk
IP23 7AW
or fax on: 01379 870 261

2 4 6 8 10 9 7 5 3 1

For Dutch. After all the years of stealing from you anyway, it's nice to finally get paid for it.

Contents

Scott Frank in conversation with Annie Nocenti

Scott Frank has a special sympatico with the work of novelist Elmore Leonard. Frank's first adaptation of a Leonard novel, *Get Shorty* (1995), earned him critical and commercial success and was nominated for Writers Guild, Golden Globe and Edgar Awards. In adapting *Out of Sight*, Frank once again demonstrates his keen affinity for Leonard's particular vision and stylistic trademarks.

Scott Frank was born in March 1960 in Fort Walton Beach, Florida. Raised in northern California, he received a BA in film studies from the University of California at Santa Barbara in 1982. While a student there, he wrote *Little Man Tate*, which became Jodie Foster's directorial debut in 1991. His other screenplays include *Dead Again* (1991, nominated for an Edgar Award), *Malice* (1993) and *Heaven's Prisoners* (1996).

Frank is in the process of adapting both Pete Dexter's *Brotherly Love* and Lawrence Block's *A Walk Among the Tombstones* for Universal Pictures. He is also writing an original screenplay entitled *The Lookout* for DreamWorks. He lives in Pasadena with his wife, their three children, and assorted animals.

In his novel Out of Sight, *Elmore Leonard presents a convict's fantasy – a romantic time-out and a successful big score – only to have it snatched away. It's clever and almost sadistic. I thought your adaptation retained Leonard's bleakness, yet gave more of a pay-off to the fantasy.*

Well, it had to be real. You couldn't have the Hollywood ending where the convict gets away. The ending in the book is the right ending – she would bust him. But you're disappointed, because you wonder: why have I gone all this way just to watch her bust him? The challenge with the ending was, how can you have that realism, but still give the audience some hope?

The novel is filled with movie references. Did you cut most of that because it felt redundant after your previous Leonard adaptation, Get Shorty, *which also uses film references?*
Yes, and because of what's happening out there with Quentin Tarantino's work and other filmmakers' work. Film characters are referencing other things, and I think that gets old very fast in film. In all of Leonard's books, his characters are always referencing some kind of pop culture, whether it's music or television or movies. Quentin Tarantino got that from Leonard.

In Out of Sight, *Leonard refers to* Three Days of the Condor *and* Bonnie and Clyde. *Talking about movies has become a kind of litmus test, or reference point, for defining character – you understand a character by the way they view a movie.*
Yes, and it's helpful. In the reshoot of the trunk scene we have the characters talk more about *Three Days of the Condor*, because it really is a parallel to the situation they're going through within that scene. It's just mentioned in the first version, and in the second version Karen actually comments on how she thought it was kind of fake the way the man and woman got together so quickly in the movie, which is exactly what's happening to them at that moment in the trunk.

That's such a key scene, and yet it takes place in the dark. Could you tell me how you approached that challenge?
My first instinct when I first read the book was – let's do it all in black. And then I thought, you can't stare at twelve minutes of black screen. So then I thought, maybe you can stare at a black screen for a minute or so, and then he can find a flashlight in amongst her junk. Because you really do need to see their faces for the scene to work. Otherwise it just becomes an exercise.

The basic problem of an adaptation has to do with lifting out an essence, and condensing without losing that essence?
I think that the key to any adaptation is to find out what the running theme of the book is. The thing with Leonard's books, and the challenge of adapting them, is that it's all so delicious. When

you begin the process, you just love everything you read. It's so much fun that you want to keep it all in the film.

So you need some sort of template, and the only template you've got is: what does this mean to me? If you're just trying to preserve the book, you get a real flat version for the movie. So you have to filter it through your own point of view and make it your own, to some degree; otherwise it has no shape. My first pass with his books has always produced long drafts. I would begin with a 180-or-so-page-long draft, where I would have virtually everything that's in the book in the script.

So you find what the book is about for you. Everything else has to fall away. In *Get Shorty*, it was the idea of everyone coming to Los Angeles to reinvent themselves. This is a city of reinvention. Whether you're a waiter who wants to be an actor, or a writer who wants to be a director, or, in the case of *Get Shorty*, a coke dealer who wants to be a producer. It's about how people are constantly looking at themselves as something other than who they are. So it's very simple – anything that isn't about that idea just falls away.

In the case of *Out of Sight*, it was about the road not taken. It was about a guy who thought: what if I hadn't been a bank robber? I could be with a woman like this, I could have that kind of life. The ongoing debate with Buddy is: it's too late for you. You are what you are. You can go home and take a shower and clean all the mud off of you and you're still a bank robber. In the book Foley was an even older character, which made it all that more poignant. In adapting the novel, anything that was not about 'the road not taken' fell away. When I looked at the scene in the trunk, that's when this idea really started to hit. You want to build to that line, 'What if things were different? What if we had met in a bar, what would happen?' And she says, 'Nothing.'

So you chose a theme that would strike a universal chord? Everyone has had that eerie feeling of a moment missed.
And yet it's sadder with him, because when you see him in prison, you see how unhappy he is, all the energy in the character is gone. It's like he cannot spend another minute in jail.

One of the symbols that played well into their differences was the continual referencing of suits. She has the expensive Chanel suit, Foley expects to be given a business suit when he goes to get a job from Ripley, but instead –
He's given a security uniform. Because suits symbolize the straight, good life. The good clean clothes as opposed to the convict uniform. And then he gets her suit all dirty!

Foley got a few guys killed by slipping in on their prison escape. You carefully left in a few key points – like that the dead men were scum and deserved to die, and how at the fence the guards would have noticed the escape anyway. But Foley's the main character and he's introduced as a snitch, which could have been a problem.
He is a snitch, but I always felt that he was a man who was desperate. All that did was speak to how badly he wanted out of prison. It didn't matter to him, he would have killed all of them himself if it meant he could get out of prison.

But a good con doesn't rat. Leonard is very complicated; he seems to be glamorizing the criminal, yet he's really making fools of them.
Yes, but I don't think there's anything glamorous about what the criminals are doing in Leonard's books. In most movies they glamorize the criminal – there's the thief in *To Catch a Thief*, there's the hitman who's untouchable and doesn't get shot, there's the bank robber who walks into a bank and is very high-tech, like the guys in *Heat*. I think that what Leonard does is he humanizes them. He brings them down to a lower level, which is more interesting. They're not looking for ten million dollars in a bank, they're trying to score anything they can.

Instead of methodically searching for valuables, they get stuck on finding a big steak in the freezer.
And suits! Steaks, suits, stereos. In the book, there isn't even any money in the house. They end up with zero, so they just begin to take anything they can get their hands on.

There's an undertone in the novel that all crooks are just dumb, and in your ending you shift that onto the character of White Boy

Bob. You were therefore able to respect Leonard's 'dumb crook' punch line, yet relieve Foley, the main character, of that stigma.
In all of Leonard's books there's the idea that the good guys are the smart crooks and the bad guys are the dumber crooks. Sometimes the bad guys will think they're smart, but what they actually have is a very specific worldview that makes them appear smart. The trick is to bring that out. What is great about Leonard's books is that he is able to get real sympathy for the 'good guy bad guys'.

The novel makes the crooks seem dumber than the script does, especially in the case of Foley and Buddy.
Foley's reason for trying this home invasion is, as he literally says in the book, 'Well, I never tried okra before either. What the hell?' It's the idea of something new, they'll give it a try.

Even though there's a price on their heads, and Maurice is gunning for them, and Karen, the federal marshal, knows they're going there. It's suicidal.
It is suicidal, and I read it as suicidal. The way I read that scene, he went in knowing this was going to be it. You can look at it entirely as a suicide mission on Foley's part, which I don't think a movie audience would go with. Or you can look at it as a realistic example of how dumb criminals are, usually. You hear stories of them accidentally shooting themselves, like what happened to White Boy Bob. The police advisor on the set said, 'You have no idea how often that happens.'

But there are smart cons, and the discrepancy in the story is that in the prison Leonard sets up Foley as a man apart. And in the end he's just as dumb.
Much like Chili Palmer [the main character in *Get Shorty*] was so disgusted with the mob life, Jack Foley was disgusted with the con life. He's got it all worked out. He was a guy, in the book, who taught other cons the ropes. He was sick of that life. In Glades in particular, he thought that there was a newer breed of con that didn't have respect for the code. He was disgusted with that. I think he looked at Chino and the others that were breaking out as

part of that new breed. That's why I never really read it as him snitching them out so much as him doing what he had to do.

By cutting the novel's subplot of the female reporter, you left Karen alone as a woman in a man's world. Also, by going right to the crime scene, you very elegantly cut to her picture in the paper, the one key plot point.
In my first draft the female reporter was there. I would have rather had the picture of Karen that is described in the book, where she's standing at the courthouse in Miami with a shotgun on her hip. But there was a page count problem and we needed to get to it faster. I found that we were convoluting things, I was creating all kinds of scenes just to get there. So I decided that what was important was not what the picture was of, but that Foley sees a picture of her.

Out of Sight *is a 'romance' where the couple meet in a trunk, and then not again for a long time. You came up with terrific ideas for how to keep them in contact.*
That was the big problem. You had two people who met for a forty-minute-or-so trunk ride, in the book, and then never see each other again until Detroit, at which point they sleep together. But all through the book they're thinking about each other. Not only that, Leonard did something smart, he gave her a prior history with a bank robber boyfriend. She likes the wild types, the cowboys, and her father constantly reminds her of that. In the novel, it worked really well. You're always in their heads, and you know that she's thinking about him and vice versa. The trick was, what to do about all the time they're not together? I thought the dream was one way, if you played it real, and yet skew it from her point of view.

The great thing about that scene is that you go into it thinking it's Foley's fantasy, but when it flips and it's her fantasy, you're caught off-guard. So you get a fantasy from both sides.
That's exactly it. I needed to do both things. It was clear that Foley liked her. There are obvious reasons why – just look at her! But

here's a guy covered in muck from the sewer, behind her in the trunk, who's charming, but you don't quite know why she'd keep thinking about him. I needed to sell it a little more. We thought it might be funny to do the dream where you're watching it and it's all slightly from a feminine point of view and you wonder: why is this guy talking about taking a hot bath? And then there's a candle in there, and there's a long conversation between him and Buddy, that we ended up cutting, where Buddy is saying, 'There's nothing like a hot bath. I'm gonna go get us some wine, and there's a vanilla candle by the tub, feel free to use it.' And you're almost thinking these two guys are gay. You're wondering, and then you realize the whole thing is from her point of view.

I bought that, I was seduced by it because it starts out as a good straight-time thing for an ex-con to do, the prisoner just out of lockup appreciates a long hot bath. It worked for me in terms of Foley just hitting the free world, right up to the vanilla candle. That's when I went, 'Huh?'

And it's a cheat, because it starts off from his point of view and ends up from her point of view. The whole idea was that you needed a piece where you saw that she was thinking about him. Where you took it for granted that she was thinking about him. And then the other thing was, you needed them to connect, for real, before he left for Detroit. And that's why I created the phone call, where he calls her up while her boyfriend was there.

In that scene you establish her willingness to be complicit. To move them closer, you had to do it physically, but also conceptually – show honour in the con and criminality in the cop.

And she's wrestling with it. She's thinking about it and resisting him but at the same time wanting him to go on. She's trying to find him, at the same time trying to play along with him.

There was a line I liked in the novel, where she asks, 'Do you have any grass?' And I thought, that's great, because that establishes criminality in her. I was surprised that was cut.

Who did she ask? I don't even remember.

She asks her dad, or he asks her, 'Got any grass?'
That's great. I'm wondering now why I cut it. [*laughs*]

Probably because there were already plenty of bits that showed that she flirts with criminality. For instance, I liked that you cut the references to the Stockholm syndrome [the tendency of a hostage to form an emotional attachment to his or her captor] because that seemed too on the money. You get it, what's happening to her, without trotting out the Stockholm syndrome.
That's interesting, because that's something that Elmore Leonard told me that he added last. It wasn't part of his first pass. He'd heard about the Stockholm syndrome, and so added it in. I thought there was a way you could play it, I thought you could use it if the father's using it to tease her. In other words, he's not telling her what the Stockholm syndrome is, but instead he's reminding her of it, to play with her.

That's true, that's good. They have a complicated relationship – the father's created her to be what she is, and then he's angry at her for being what she is. He gives her a present of a gun and then he says, don't play with cowboys.
Exactly. Except in the book you don't see him give her the gun.

You put the gift into the present tense, which I loved. Many of your created scenes spun out of clues in the novel.
That's always the challenge, and what he does is he gives you such great characters that it's easy to infer from them. There's so much juice in these characters that it's always really easy to add more plot. You just go back to the characters and think, what would they do? Well, Foley would call her up.

Leonard talks about how plot is not that important to him. He's said, 'I just kind of drag plot in.'
Plot is no fun for him. He doesn't like to know where he's going when he sits down every day. He just wants to see what happens. So the other trick with adapting him is that you have to give structure to happenstance. His books just unfold. Basically it's: shit happens. So you're always trying to find out which story

you're going to tell, and then structure it accordingly.

Also, he's an ensemble character writer, and that juice you spoke of is between the characters. It's not solo performances so much as it is keeping that tension between characters.
And it's also about unpredictability. You never know what someone's going to do, and people misconstrue what someone else is trying to do and then react accordingly. So things are always happening out of left field or happening suddenly. People are impetuous in his books in a great way. They just decide to do something, and it changes everything. It works great.

You opened with the bank robbery, I assume, so that the film would open in a more active way?
Yes, but I opened with the bank robbery also because it was a great way to set up the character. I thought, if you met him under those circumstances you would be charmed by him, you'd want him to break out of prison, you would go with him anywhere.

The time loop you added into the linear narrative was wonderful, when you return to the moment he rips his tie off, feel his frustration and know why he robbed the bank in the opening scene. Leonard doesn't plot that way.
No, but what he does do is that he will often describe the same event and build up to it from three different points of view. He'll play with structure that way.

What differences have you discovered, between the language of the novel and the language of film?
I think the difference is more in the storytelling than it is in the language. I think screenplays are more terse than novels. You have to say a lot with a little because you don't have the time to set the scene the way you do in a book. But I think the fundamental difference is that in the storytelling in a novel you have time to digress, you don't always have to move in a straight line. In a screenplay, everything has to be on-story. If you're off-story at all, unless it's really interesting, it kills the momentum of the movie. You have to be very careful. Sometimes you can do it, if the movie

is set up in such a way that the rules are that anything can happen. But for the stories I like to tell, I find that in the movie, if you get off the story it really hurts. I find that limiting, also. I find that I want to tell the characters' stories.

So if you find yourself going off on a segue, you'd better make sure that it continues the sense of underlying story?
You'd better be sure that it has narrative energy. That you're moving forward. That you're not just stopping to have a flashback about a character, unless it has something to do with the story.

The scene with Karen's boyfriend and her father would have felt too disgressionary if you hadn't added in that phone call from Foley.
That's exactly it, there's no reason for it otherwise. All you're doing is introducing this guy. It was in the script for a draft or two without the phone call. It set up Karen's relationship with her father, but it had nothing to do with the plot. It did set up that she was thinking about Foley, but nothing moved forward.

One of the wonderful things you created that wasn't in the novel was the fish storyline. What inspired that whole riff?
The riff with the fish is more in the screenplay than in the film. The fish are still a part of Ripley's life, but he doesn't go into the long speech about why he's so into fish. Which I miss, but it didn't seem to play onscreen. Those scenes came at places in the movie when you're really into the story between Jack Foley and Karen, you want to know what's going to happen between them.

And yet your initial inspiration to give that relationship some meat was right on, because, for one thing, Ripley isn't even in the end of the novel; he needed story.
That's right, and I felt also that Foley needed a more personal reason to go rob Ripley, to go after this guy. I think that I might not have found the most efficient way of telling that story. I think that while you're reading something, you have a different set of criteria for how you're going to absorb what's happening. Whereas when you watch something, you really are much more anxious for things to keep moving.

In the script, the fish obsession is extremely effective. Because you really get the sense, not only of Ripley being this white-collar criminal, but that he's more amoral than Foley, and you see that when he's talking about fish.
The other thing I wanted to establish with Ripley, and I don't know if I succeeded or not, is the whole notion of fate. Ripley was really into fate. If I'm supposed to be here, so be it. Fate coming out of, I think, guilt. I thought that would be interesting, to have that be Foley's take on events at the end of the film. The problem was, there wasn't enough time to tell that story as completely as it needed to be told. They become scenes where you just wanted to get the impression of what's going on and get right back to Jack and Karen. Which was a good lesson for me.

Did you have to figure out what number of references to fish would be perfect, so that when Foley sees the fish tank in the end, you think, 'Aha!' as opposed to, 'I saw that coming.'
That's the hard thing. There's always someone who says, 'I knew the diamonds were going to be in the fish tank.' I also felt, in some ways, that I didn't care if people knew. I just thought it should be funny. And not that funny, given that fish represent this pure thing to Ripley yet that's where he hides all his money.

A smart story change was to put all the players together at the Lompac prison, because it condensed a lot of story.
Even though it's not real, a white-collar criminal wouldn't have been in jail with those guys. But I thought there were too many different prisons in the story, and people were in prison at different times. It was hard for me to keep it straight, in the book. I thought the only thing to do was to visually see them there, in one prison, all together.

It set your stage, and flipped the protection scam. Foley stopped Maurice's scam, which added tension between them.
That's correct, whereas in the novel Foley and Maurice didn't even know each other.

There's also a couple things in the novel that don't make sense. I don't think you can walk or drive up to a prison fence at night, without having tower-guard rifles turned on you. Leonard almost opens with an apology for that in the novel, knowing it's unrealistic.
The other thing is that black and white cons don't mix. And yet in the yard, we have Foley and Buddy hanging out. In the novel, Buddy is a white redneck.

That worked for me, because there's a certain kind of con that transcends the gang mentality.
Ving Rhames, who plays Buddy, was very concerned with that. He wanted to know why they would be friends, why he would hang out with this guy. Which is why we created the story of how they met, in front of the bank, which we ultimately cut from the film. Again, some of it is just in the name of pace. You're watching where a scene gets bogged down and so you lift things out. I found that I think people need more information than they actually do, when they watch a movie. People get things a lot faster. That's why I'm often frustrated by the screenwriting format. You can't tell everything you want to tell. Because it's not something that's meant to be read, it's something that's meant to be looked at later. I love all that stuff that ultimately may or may not matter once it's on film. But at a certain point you have to be ruthless, and you have to decide what's helping the movie and what's just playing flat. It's hard. We lost a lot of stuff that I love.

Because you're listening to a higher principle. I had an editor once who would say, 'Always edit out your favorite lines, because they're the ones that aren't right.' I never even wanted to quite comprehend that.
[*Laughs*] It's true, you're watching and there are things you thought were going to be so hysterical or powerful and you watch them go right by. And then there are things that you hadn't given a second thought to that turn out to be the biggest moments in the movie.

For instance, the tuna casserole story. Love is funny.
Which we cut. I loved it because it was thematically part of this

movie. Love is funny, it's the whole thing. But again, it's at a point in the movie when you don't want to stop. That was one of my favorite scenes. Every chance I got, I would put it in, and Steven Soderbergh kept cutting it out. Because he knew that at that point you're going to be driving, and you're not going to want to stop and have a moment.

It's interesting. Because part of me says, I'd rather stop. I don't know that I need to be driven.
I agree with you, and I think that movies go too fast now. I think movies now don't take the time to define character. Basically, what they do is set up an attitude for a given person and then go with it. But, at the same time, I think we've also reached a point where a lot of movies, especially the movies of younger directors, have become totally self-indulgent. They have scenes in their films that are only in there because the director loves them. They would keep all those scenes we're talking about. And yeah, they're all great scenes, but what you end up with is something that plays at the same level. I really do feel that a good story has a certain rhythm to it, that just because a scene in and of itself is a good scene doesn't mean it's serving that rhythm. And that's hard to tell until you see it cut into the movie. When you're reading, you're focusing on one scene at a time, as individual scenes, and it's hard to tell where the movie is going to drag.

One idea in the novel was the convict's fantasy of the big score. The scene you added, that I think was key, was when they're talking in the car, and Foley says, 'But does anybody ever get the big score?' Leonard would say, no. Would you say, let's at least entertain the idea?
I would say, no, but you can dream about it. And I think that every movie is predicated on the big score. That we're going to get the big score, or that we're going to do something, that we're all going to try. And for some reason everyone tries, for the same reason everyone buys lottery tickets.

In the sense that movies are impossible possibilities? They are romanticized, and you fed this story back into that myth?
The other reason I did that was to show that Foley is realistic about what might happen to him. He's not expecting to go off and live on an island somewhere. That whole discussion builds to the notion of, 'All I know is, I'm not going back to jail.' And Buddy saying, 'They put a gun on you, you're going back to jail.' And Foley saying, 'They put a gun on you, you still have a choice.' That's the key to that whole scene.

On the stairs, at the end, Foley has his Clyde Barrow movie moment. In the book, the minute Karen stops believing in their fantasy, it's over. There's more of a sense that she's looking at him with pity, whereas you keep the fantasy going.
What Leonard did at the end was real, given that these lowlifes are in this house, and that Foley was with them. But in reading the book, it was the only time where I lost sympathy for the character. I did think he was pathetic, I was embarrassed for him being around a lowlife like Snoopy. I didn't want her to see him around Snoopy. So I needed, in the screenplay, to create a really good reason for him to go there. And Snoopy is the obstacle. He's not there with Snoopy, they were going to go in ahead of him. But Snoopy, who at that point is calling himself Maurice, decided to go in a day ahead also. So now they have to do it together.

And you also gave Foley a score to settle with Ripley, who humiliated Foley after Foley saved him in prison.
That's right, it was more about that. The same thing with the crackhouse in the book. There's that long sequence in the book where [Snoopy and his cohorts] go into the crackhouse.

I was surprised you didn't use that, because it's a filmic, active scene. And yet the way you cut it was wonderful, because you just switched the POV and showed their mania by showing its aftermath, through Glenn's fear and Karen seeing the wreckage.
There was one version we had written where you hear all of it. You're in the crackhouse, but you're just on Glenn, listening. And

during reshoots, we ended up putting that scene back into the movie. Again, it was a rhythm thing, it felt weird not to go there at all, to just talk about it. It's one of the best-written scenes in the book, it's so powerful. But it's just so dark, it would take you out of the movie. If you see that in the movie, and Foley spends even one minute with these people, you'll lose all sympathy with him.

Was there a time when you entertained killing Buddy like he's killed in the novel?
Right up until the very last draft. He was killed in the script, and at the last minute [*producer*] Danny DeVito said to me: we just can't kill this guy. You like the character so much, it's such a left turn to kill him, given the way the movie's evolved.

Foley going to prison and Buddy dying was too much of a double downer?
It becomes awful. It was one of those things where I was kicking myself for not having thought of it earlier. But Danny was right, because then, if you have Buddy get away with all the money, it makes great sense, especially given all Buddy's religious leanings.

Because it's not only hope, but it spirals back thematically into the notion of fantasizing.
The big score! It's the whole punch line for Foley's line, 'No one ever gets the big score.' Buddy naively gets the big score. Again, in the book, the way Buddy was killed is very strong, much the way the crackhouse is very strong. I just felt that for audiences, having invested so much in these people, to get the rug pulled out from under them was too much. And onscreen, they're alive in a way that they're not in the book.

Leonard can set a bleak tone, give things an ironic, dark edge, so that when he makes these left turns into severe violence you go with it. Whereas filmically, you can't quite –
People don't necessarily stay with you. I felt that the book ending was absolutely right for the book. That was what was so scary to me. How do you come up with an ending that doesn't compromise the ending of the book, that doesn't turn it into a fake Hollywood

uplifting ending, how do you come up with something that's in between?

What's brilliant about your ending is that you picked up on two little clues in the book that suggest a happier ending. There's the running questions about how a magician does his tricks. And then there's the line that the father, as a joke, says to Karen, 'Gee, maybe you'll get to take Foley to prison.' So you took those clues and came up with an escape artist as the second convict, along with Foley, that she has to transport.

In my first draft of the script, I really thought she should bust him, and that should be the end of it. I think that was more a rationalization on my part for keeping what's there rather than doing the heavy lifting that's required to come up with a new ending. I was having this conversation with Leonard about the end of the movie, about going off to prison, about how bleak that is, and about how I can't do that. And he just started telling me, out of the blue, about these letters he got from this guy in prison who had busted out of prison eleven times. And all of a sudden, there was the ending of the movie! I stopped him and said, no, wait! Tell me about that guy! I made him a Muslim in the screenplay, he isn't in real life. I thought it was some sort of kismet, given where I was at in the script at that moment.

You also added in the murder, when Maurice kills in prison. Was that to establish how tough he was?

I wanted to establish Maurice at the top of the movie, so I put in the fight, too, and the boxing, to establish Maurice as a fighter. And the other thing was to make the threat from this guy real. Because when you meet him in the novel, he's throwing a fight. So that almost hurts you, in establishing the character.

Another cut was the hobo camp, and the plotline of what Chino did after the prison escape.

We didn't have time. Again, the point of the movie was the road not taken. This guy wanting this girl. Foley wants to no longer rob banks, because he wants to no longer be in prison, yet the irony is he's going to rip off this guy to make that happen. The hobo camp was really interesting, and it also established Chino as a violent guy. In the movie he's a bit more of a buffoon, the way the actor decided to play him. In the script, I wanted him to be dangerous. And then during rehearsal, I'd always loved the scene where she puts the gun on him, and he has the gun on Adele. It's a really nice scene, because he puts the gun down simply because he believes she might shoot him. It's a great moment. But the police advisor on the set, he said that would never happen. We ended up rechoreographing the scene so that he gets stuck in the door. All this stuff happens, all to justify reality. And I feel, if something's realistic, that's good enough, it doesn't have to be real. As long as it doesn't take you out of the movie, or seem absurd. I thought that scene was very strong. He puts the gun down and says, 'I believe she would have shot me.' It's a much stronger scene. Now, he's a buffoon, and he's on the floor and he's ad-libbing lines like, 'I gotta make pee-pee.' The actor is ad-libbing all this stuff and the audience loves it. I sat in the back of the theatre and I couldn't believe it.

So was the police advisor both helpful and detrimental?
I think he was very helpful, but because they know the world so well, they want it to be the way it plays out in the real world. I feel like oftentimes, what's real or true to life isn't entertaining. It would have been great for Chino and Karen to have that scene the way I wrote it, and it's silly now, but I have to say audiences love it, so maybe I'm wrong. Maybe the advisor saved the scene.

Why did you switch Foley's weapon during the escape from a board to a crucifix?
It ended up, in the film, being a heavy vase. Danny DeVito was afraid we'd get in trouble from the religious community.

I thought it was a good, dark touch. What does the title Out of Sight *refer to? That the fantasy was out of Foley's sights?*
I don't know. Maybe hiding? That people are hiding? I couldn't figure it out. When Leonard was writing the novel, his first title

was 'Crook of the Year'. Because someone, I think it was Ivan Boesky, was on the cover of *Newsweek* or somewhere as crook of the year. I always assumed *Out of Sight* meant that everyone was hiding from everyone else. Which is probably wrong.

What did you think of Jackie Brown, *Quentin Tarantino's adaptation of Leonard's novel* Rum Punch?
It was a good adaptation, and a very good movie. If I had any criticism at all, it would be that Tarantino hadn't decided, for himself, what it was about. Everything that was in the book was in the movie. He didn't pick that one thematic element. I felt the story didn't add up to enough to be a three-hour movie. Scene for scene, they're interesting, well-drawn scenes. It's well directed and well acted, but ultimately you don't know what it was about. Is it about him and her, is it about the job, is it about a man tired of being a bail bondsman? You don't really know. I understand why he did what he did, he wanted it to be a pure Elmore Leonard movie. And it is. But the problem with pure Elmore Leonard is that it's without thematic structure. And movies have to have structure. The scenes don't serve a central idea.

Steven Soderbergh's an interesting director, because he's so devoted to the notion of experimenting in film.
I think he'll always be experimenting. He's very adventurous, and unafraid to try things. He's realistic about the business of film-making, and how you get to do what you want to do, but at the same time he's really true to himself. Also, he's very collaborative. He never shut out the producers, the actors, or myself. He was open to hearing ideas, not that he'd necessarily use them. In the love scene, when we were watching dallies, everyone was saying, you didn't go far enough. And he kept saying, wait till you see it cut. He resisted reshooting, and he was right. And there were times when he was wrong. He shot the trunk scene in real time, in one take. It was a great idea, but it didn't quite work, and he was the first one to say, let's change the approach.

He thought the one take would heighten the claustrophobic nature of the scene?
Yes. He thought he would put you in the trunk with them. It was a good idea. It was my first instinct, as a screenwriter, to write it that way. So working with Steven was one of those rare experiences. Even though it was a shotgun marriage to begin with, we saw the same movie.

In your last interview with Scenario, *when we published* Get Shorty, *you mentioned that before you direct, you want to write a novel.*
I have a third of it down, but it's hard to steal the time. I just bought a new house, and I'm a slave to it. This year, July 4th, I keep saying, will be my Independence Day. I'll take a few months to drop out of the movie business and finish it.

Is successful screenwriting a golden rut for writers who would like to try other forms?
I like writing screenplays, but I'm feeling limited by the form. I want to tell the whole story this time. I'm also very collaborative, I listen to everybody when I work on a film, and the only way to jettison all the other voices, to save my own, is to write a novel.

Is your novel influenced by Leonard?
I don't see how it couldn't be. I've spent the last couple of years adapting him. I think he's sort of seeped into my wheelhouse.

This interview first appeared in *Scenario*, vol. 4, no. 2, Summer 1998.

Steven Soderbergh on *Out of Sight*

The joys and charms of an Elmore Leonard novel – haphazard, jigsaw plots, impetuous digressions, flickering time shifts, juicy bit players – become challenges for those who wish to translate his work to the screen. Director Steven Soderbergh has always been devoted to experimentation, and was able to draw on his repertoire of techniques, including distinct color shifts for each locale and time frame, camera tremors and freeze frames, to handle these challenges.

Soderbergh says he was first attracted to *Out of Sight* because of 'an odd, fatalistic tone that I responded to and wanted to portray. Clearly, my aesthetic as a filmmaker was going to come across in the visual language of the film, but I wanted to do everything in my power to enhance that feeling I had when I first read the script.'

For the freeze frames, which sometimes were cues to time shifts, and other times just emphasized a moment, Soderbergh used an instinctive approach. 'I didn't have a formula. I didn't follow any real logic and in that regard I was like Leonard – I just went with it when I felt it was appropriate. It's also a comment, it's a signal that says: remember this moment. It was a gimmick I always liked when it began to be employed by the French and British New Wave, and then it got appropriated by television and done to death. I hadn't seen it in a while, and felt it was a nice way to comment on something.'

Soderbergh also employed an almost subliminal tremor in the bar scene, to heighten the sense of attraction between Karen Sisco and Jack Foley. 'I decided to go hand-held, but not in a flashy way, just to give it that trembling sensation.' As that scene segues into the bedroom, Soderbergh inter-cuts time frames with disjointed voiceover, as if the love scene were already a memory. This, in turn, reminds us that this doomed liaison hinges on an impossible possibility, and is, perhaps, still just a fantasy.

A distinct color palette was created for each scene – icy blues in

Detroit, pop bubble-gum colors for Adele's home, washed-out prison yards – to help give footing during the complex time shifts. There was also a large supporting cast to embrace. 'The key to the ensemble was to cast actors that don't comment on their performance as they're giving it. What makes Leonard's characters so funny is their lack of self-awareness. If you have an actor who is essentially sitting with the audience watching the performance as they're giving it, you're dead. Everyone we cast understood that. They're so present, as characters, and they so lack perspective, that they're comical.' These various techniques, used in tandem, helped reinforce the viewers' footing during the wild, nonlinear, time-looped narrative ride. 'Hopefully,' says Soderbergh, 'they create an overall effect of looseness, and a feeling of freedom. I wanted the movie, stylistically, to be very loose. I didn't want it to be as formal as some of my other work has been.'

In prior films, especially *Schizopolis* (1996), Soderbergh used the medium to comment on itself, to provoke, to question form, to be, as he once said, 'agitprop'. '*Schizopolis* is a seriously deconstructed film. What's great about having just employed a sort of Jackson Pollock method is that the films that followed benefited from that explosion of ideas. I came away thinking: Well, I don't want to go *that* far again, but there are things I can appropriate and an energy I want to keep. It's a part of the process that's hard to indulge, because of the cutthroat nature of the business. It is a business, but it's also an art. The people who are at the forefront of experimentation get hammered a bit, but make it easier for the rest of us to follow. I certainly don't think I've been at the forefront of anything, but within my own little niche, I keep trying to push as much as I can. Somebody's gotta hurl the javelin and see where it lands. Then you can say: Huh. I don't want to throw it *that* far. We need people out there excavating the edges to find out how much further we can go. We can't stand still.'

Once Soderbergh developed his approach – applying, more judiciously, the stylistic techniques pioneered in his earlier work – it was time to have fun. 'Our intent was just to spin a good yarn. The spine of the movie was solid. I had a backbone that allowed me to digress without losing the audience. That's what Leonard is about, wonderful digressions. Directorially, I can get away with that if there's a backbone, a motor that drives the movie on a very definitive path. I can riff, because I know what the twelve-bar sequence is that holds the movie together. That's a great feeling.'

A low-down, tough-luck, urban heist film, *Out of Sight* is also largely a romance, and Soderbergh allowed the fast pace to skid to a halt for intimate moments between Karen Sisco and Jack Foley. 'A lion's share of the movie relied on the chemistry between the two of them, and whether you believed that they would be obsessed with each other.' And yet, it's also irrepressibly romance Leonard-style. 'That's what I loved about the script. She shot him. That's what has to happen. You have two people on a collision course, and I was so pleased that there wasn't a hollow epiphany at that point that enabled them to skirt the confrontation. When I read the last five pages of the script, I knew that I was going to go after it.'

By having scenes flicker between prison and the outside world, Soderbergh was able to create a sense of the reality of a career criminal. To heighten that sense of being trapped, even while Foley was on the outside, Soderbergh placed him in settings that emphasized this. For instance, Foley is in a car in one scene, and a spidering shadow of tree branches covers the car, birds screeching in the distance. 'Foley's life is very confined. His fatalism insures that he will be confined, one way or another. I was always looking for opportunities to cage him. To surround him with an environment that was unsettling. The transition out of the last Ripley flashback, with the contrast between that sunny Miami feel, and then a cut to the cold, monochromatic close-up of him, and then a jump-cut further out, of him just sitting there in the car, is one of my favorites in the movie.'

While filming, he realized that there was a gender reversal happening. 'Sisco's got more of the guy's part and Foley's got more of the woman's part. He's following his heart and doesn't care where it leads him. She's a hard-ass. At the end of the day her work is more important to her. She shoots him, and walks away. That's more typically a guy thing to do. There's a role reversal there. Jack's the one sitting around pining, and exposing himself emotionally.'

Soderbergh also had fun with the star cameos. The character of Ray Nicolet was also in Quentin Tarantino's film *Jackie Brown* (an adaptation of Leonard's *Rum Punch*), and both times Nicolet was played by Michael Keaton. 'As far as Tarantino and I could determine, that's a first. I don't think that's ever been done before, where two unrelated movies share a character that is played by the same actor in both. We all giggled at that.' Sam Jackson has a star turn at the very end of the film. 'It's a short scene, so we needed someone that, when they implied that they were the preeminent escape artist in the country, you believed them right away. It had to be somebody with that kind of impact. Sam Jackson gets on screen, and says something, and you go: Whatever you say.'

Sometimes genres collide in the film, as in the tense, drawing-room farce of the climactic scene in Ripley's house. 'That was borderline Restoration comedy and suspense movie. That was the way Scott Frank and I envisioned it. It has people going in and out of doors, we've got the steaks, and the safe with nothing in it, it all seemed comedic. And as crooks, they're such amateurs. As soon as it turns out that the diamonds are not lying there on a plate for them, they fall apart.'

When asked what part of making *Out of Sight* was the most fun, Soderbergh said, 'When Scott and I went through the script inch by inch, those weeks when we were spitballing it, playing around with it. We beat it up. We kept hammering at it. At that point it's all possibilities. You're just bouncing things back and forth trying to top each other. Without the hundred and fifty people that you will have tethered to your belt once you start shooting. You're just sitting there musing and riffing.'

Will they collaborate again? 'I would kill to do a movie like *Murder on the Orient Express*. A multi-character mystery. Scott and I are absolutely nuts about that kind of a movie, and he's the guy to write it.' – *Annie Nocenti*

This piece first appeared in *Scenario*, vol. 4, no. 2, Summer 1998.

Out of Sight

BLACK

We hear traffic, some street noises, then . . .

FADE IN:

EXT. MIAMI STREET. DAY

The financial district. Lots of people in suits. A shaky, spasmodic zoom-in finds . . .

Jack Foley – forty, big, focused expression – as he rips a tie from around his neck and throws it down in the gutter. He starts across the street, now peeling off his suitcoat and dropping that, too, right there on the asphalt as we then . . .

Pan over to a bank across the street as Foley goes inside.

CUT TO:

A printed brochure that reads:

LOOKING FOR MONEY?
YOU'VE COME TO THE RIGHT PLACE.

We then pull back to reveal . . .

INT. BANK. DAY

Foley stands at a counter holding the above Credit Application while he studies the bank layout.

He watches a man in a suit, carrying an attaché case, enter the bank and move through the gate into the fenced-off business area at the front. An executive rises from his desk, shakes hands with the man and they both sit down.

Foley tosses the brochure in the trash, then crosses to a teller window where a nameplate on the counter tells us the young woman with the pile of dark hair smiling at him is Loretta.

TELLER/LORETTA

How can I help you, sir?

FOLEY

Loretta, you see that guy talking to your manager, has his case open?

Foley takes out a Zippo lighter and casually, yet expertly, begins to fiddle with it as the teller looks across the bank.

LORETTA

That's Mr Guindon, one of our assistant managers. Our manager is Mr Schoen, but he's not in today.

FOLEY

But you see the guy with the attaché case?

LORETTA

(*looks again*)

Yes.

FOLEY

That's my partner. He has a gun in there. And if you don't do exactly what I tell you, or you give me any kind of a problem, I'll look over at my partner and he'll shoot your Mr Guindon between the eyes.

Loretta goes stiff, swallows, stares back at Foley.

Now take one of those big envelopes and put as many hundreds, fifties and twenties as you can pack into it. Nothing with bank straps or rubber bands. I don't want any dye packs. I don't want any bait money. Start with the second drawer and then the one over there, under the computer. Come on, Loretta, the key's right there next to you. No bills off the bottom of the drawer.

(*as she works*)

First time being robbed?

(*she nods*)

You're doing great. Just smile, Loretta, so you won't look like you're being held up.

(*she smiles awkwardly*)

That's the way, you're doing fine.

We hear a bit of thunder and Foley cuts a fast look out the front door. When he turns back, he sees that Loretta's having some trouble fitting all the bills into the envelope.

FOLEY

Here, give me the twenties. I'll put 'em in my pocket. OK, I haven't had to give my partner a sign; that's good. Now, he's gonna wait thirty seconds till after I'm out the door, make sure you haven't set off the alarm. If you have, he's gonna shoot Mr Guindon between the eyes. OK? I think that'll do it. Thank you, Loretta, and have a nice day.

LORETTA

You, too.

Foley heads for the door. He pauses by Mr Guindon's desk, looks back at Loretta. Foley smiles at her, then turns to the man sitting with Mr Guindon, indicates Loretta . . .

FOLEY

She's cute, isn't she?

The man looks across the bank at Loretta.

MAN

Uh, yeah, I guess so.

Foley winks at Loretta and walks out.

(*to Mr Guindon*)

Who was that?

EXT. BANK. DAY

As Foley comes out, he calmly walks to a Honda Civic and gets in.

INT. CAR. DAY

Foley tries to start the car. No go. He tries again.

FOLEY

Come on . . .

But the car won't start. Foley bangs on the wheel.

Fuck!

Foley then stiffens as a cop sticks his gun through the open window into Foley's ear.

COP

I think you flooded it.

Foley looks to the passenger window, where another cop, smiling, now has his gun pointing at him.

SECOND COP

Get out've the car, sir.

FOLEY

Wanna hear a funny story?

SECOND COP

Shut up and get out of the car.

And as Foley obliges, we then . . .

FADE TO WHITE

We hear a man grunt. Then see Foley in slow motion as he jumps through frame; now we see a basketball come up in his hand as we realize he's on his way to the rim when . . .

Another guy rams into him in mid-air, knocks him down.

EXT. PRISON YARD. DAY

A basketball game in progress. All of the men, Foley included, are dressed in blue coveralls and white T-shirts. The game is rough. Hair is pulled. Eyes are poked. Faces punched.

A title reads: GLADES CORRECTIONAL INSTITUTION. BELLE GLADE, FLORIDA.

Foley is the oldest player here. He's getting tired, starts to lose his breath. He finally walks off the court, breathing so hard he can't even talk. He simply motions to some young convict to come in and take his place.

Foley sits down on a bench, tries to catch his breath. He looks across the yard to where a group of elderly inmates sitting around a wooden picnic table are playing cards. All of them are over sixty. One of them, a one-legged guy on crutches, hops away from the table, spits out some tobacco.

Intercut the old-timers with Foley watching them.

One old guy is making a picture frame out of old Pall Mall and Lucky Strike packets. Another tends to a tomato bush in a tiny patch of garden near the wall. Another one sits nearby, painting a picture of a man and a boy fishing from a rowing boat.

Foley is about to get up off the bench when something catches his eye. He watches as two Latino men, both little guys, jog past the game, slow to a walk, then stop and begin stretching out. One of them nods to Foley. Foley nods back, waits for the Latin guys to walk off, then walks over to a guard, Pupko ('Pup'), heavy-set, dumb as dirt.

PUP

You want something, Foley?

Foley keeps his eyes fixed on the basketball game.

FOLEY

Some people are going out of here. What if I told you where and when?

PUP

How many?

FOLEY

I expect you to look out for me, Pup, let me run off work details.

PUP

OK. How many going out?

FOLEY

I hear six.

PUP

When?

FOLEY

Looks like tonight.

PUP

You know who they are?

FOLEY

I do, but I won't tell you just yet. Meet me in the chapel at eight-thirty, right before lock-down.

INT. MESS HALL. DAY

As Foley takes his lunch tray up the centre aisle, he scans the sea of white T-shirts until he sees the two little Latins sitting at a table full of other little Latins. Chino – fifties, in shape – shovels macaroni in his mouth.

Chino's 'wife', Lulu, nineteen, looks up from his own neat tray of macaroni and jello and watches Foley walk past and sit down with a bunch of bikers.

Foley watches as the guy across from Chino scrapes some macaroni off his plate and on to Chino's and Chino wolfs that down, too.

EXT. MESS. DAY

Chino steps outside and lights a cigarette. He puts an arm around Lulu, starts to walk off . . .

FOLEY

(*off-screen*)

Today's the day, huh?

Chino looks over, watches Foley approach, lets his arm slip down so he can hook his thumb into Lulu's belt – the next thing to having him on a leash.

You excited?

CHINO

I told you, man, Super Bowl Sunday.

FOLEY

Yeah, but I see you moved it up.

CHINO

(*beat*)

Why you think is today?

FOLEY

You were out running this morning, sticking to your routine, anybody happened to notice. But you only did a couple of miles instead of your usual five. Saving yourself for the main event. Then I see you inside eating ten pounds of macaroni. Carbohydrates for endurance.

Chino and Lulu exchange looks.

CHINO

You want, I tole you you can come. You all right, Foley. I like you.

FOLEY

You told me I can come 'cause I caught you digging the fuckin' tunnel, saw you and Lulu coming out of the bushes, thought maybe you two were making out.

Foley smiles at Lulu, who glares back at him.

So what, you finish ahead of schedule?

Chino looks towards the fence along the front of the yard.

CHINO

You see what they doing, those posts out there? Putting up another fence, five metres on the other side of the one that's there. We wait until Super Bowl Sunday, they could have the second fence built and we have to dig another nine, ten days. So we going soon as it's dark. You want – I mean it – you can still come.

FOLEY

I appreciate the offer. And it's tempting.

Foley looks off towards the visitors' parking area, the fence not twenty yards away.

But, man, it's a long run to civilization. A hundred miles to Miami? I'm too old to start acting crazy, try a stunt like that. You make it out, send me a postcard.

CUT TO:

A notepad where we see someone has written 'IT'S MAGIC!' *then crossed out the* 'IT'S' *and replaced it with the word* 'LIKE'. *We hear the phone ring and . . .*

INT. ADELE'S APARTMENT. DAY

Miami Beach Moderne. Adele – mid-thirties, pretty, Foley's ex – sits at her kitchen table writing on a pad. She grabs the phone.

ADELE

Hello?

(*then sighs*)

Yeah, I accept.

INT. PRISON HALLWAY. DAY

Foley on the phone.

FOLEY'S VOICE

Hey, Adele, how you doing?

Intercutting Foley and Adele:

ADELE

Hey, Bank Robber, want some advice? Next time, leave the engine running.

FOLEY

That's funny, Adele. How many more times you gonna gimme that one?

ADELE

Till it's not funny any more. What do you want, Jack?

FOLEY

You know that Super Bowl party? They changed the date. It's on *tonight*, eight-thirty.

ADELE

Didn't you tell me one-time calls aren't monitored?

FOLEY

I said not as a rule.

ADELE

So why don't you come right out and tell me what you're talking about?

FOLEY

Listen to Miss Smarty Mouth. Out there in the free world.

ADELE

What's free about it? I'm looking for work.

FOLEY

What happened to Mandrake the Magician?

ADELE

Emil the Amazing. The bastard fired me and hired another

girl, a redhead. I'm working on a new business card, pass out to the cafés. How's this sound –

FOLEY

(*cuts her off*)

Listen, Adele, the reason I called, that party is today instead of Sunday. About eight-thirty, like only a few hours from now. So you'll have to get hold of Buddy, whatever he might be doing.

ADELE

And the one driving the other car?

FOLEY

What're you talking about?

ADELE

Well, seeing as you have so much luck with cars, Buddy thought it might be better to bring two. He got this guy he says you know from Lompoc, Glenn something.

FOLEY

Glenn Michaels.

ADELE

Yeah, that's him. Buddy says Glenn thinks you guys are real cool.

FOLEY

He did, huh. Well, tell Buddy I see Glenn wearing his sunglasses, I'll step on 'em. I might not even take 'em off first.

INT. RESTAURANT. DAY

Marshall Sisco – fifty – slides a small wrapped box across a table . . .

MARSHALL

Happy birthday.

. . . to where Karen Sisco – twenty-eight, black suit, long hair, a knockout – sits. She picks up the box and shakes it.

KAREN

You fit another Chanel suit in here?

MARSHALL

Something better. Open it.

Karen starts to carefully unwrap the present. Marshall watches, takes a sip of his drink, looks around the bar, sees how everyone's looking at the two of them . . .

KAREN

(*opens the box*)

Oh my God . . .

She pulls a gleaming automatic pistol from the box . . .

It's beautiful.

MARSHALL

It's a –

KAREN

– Sig-Sauer .38. I love it.

She leans across the table and kisses him.

Thanks, Dad.

MARSHALL

Happy birthday, kid.

(*pause*)

You want another Coke?

KAREN

(*checks her watch*)

Can't. I gotta drive out to Glades, then I'm meeting Ray Nicolet at ten.

MARSHALL

Which one is that? The ATF guy?

KAREN

He was. Ray's with the FBI now, he switched over.

MARSHALL

He's still married though, huh?

KAREN

Technically. They're separated.

MARSHALL

Oh, he's moved out?

KAREN

He's about to.

MARSHALL

Then they're not separated, are they?

KAREN

Can we change the subject?

MARSHALL

What're you doing at Glades?

KAREN

Serving process, a Summons and Complaint. Some con doing mandatory life doesn't like macaroni and cheese. He files suit, says he has no choice in what they serve and it violates his civil rights.

MARSHALL

You know you can always step in, work with me full-time as one of my investigators.

KAREN

No thanks.

MARSHALL

You used to like it.

KAREN

Dad . . .

MARSHALL

You'd meet doctors, lawyers – nothing wrong with them necessarily if they're divorced. Why settle for some cowboy cop who drinks too much and cheats on his wife? That's the way those hotshots are, all of 'em.

KAREN

I really gotta go.

MARSHALL

We don't get to talk much any more.

KAREN

How 'bout I come next Sunday and watch the Super Bowl with you?

MARSHALL

I'd like that.

She gets up, kisses him again.

KAREN

Thanks for the gun, Dad.

INT. FOLEY'S CELL. BELLE GLADE. DAY

Foley comes in, lies down on the bunk. He looks about the cell. All he's got to show for himself. It's now quiet on the cellblock. He closes his eyes.

CUT TO:

A PRISON AUDITORIUM

A few hundred cons scream encouragement/insults as Maurice 'Snoopy' Miller, a lanky, scary, mean-looking black man in boxing trunks, hits a white guy with a ferocious hook.

A title reads: LOMPOC FEDERAL PENITENTIARY, LOMPOC, CALIFORNIA. *And then:* TWO YEARS AGO.

At the back of the auditorium Foley leans in a doorway watching with Buddy Bragg – black, Foley's age, shaved head.

The bell sounds and the white guy staggers to his corner, as does Maurice. Glenn Michaels – surfer look, dark shades – counts cash in Maurice's corner, whispers something into the fighter's ear.

BUDDY

Ref don't call it pretty soon, Snoopy's gonna send this guy out in a body bag.

Foley watches a man – fifties, out of place, not as hard-looking as those around him. The guy looks nervous, can feel the other cons' eyes on him as he tries to find a seat.

The bell sounds and the white boxer staggers to his feet. Maurice steps in and resumes the bloody pummelling. Foley turns and watches the fight now.

FOLEY

Anyone ever tell you why they call him Snoopy?

Buddy shakes his head. Maurice dances around the other guy now. Teases him.

He was Maurice 'Mad Dog' Miller back when he was pro. Now you pet him, he goes down.

The white guy throws a tired, loping roundhouse that barely glances off Maurice's jaw. Sure enough, Maurice makes a big show out of snapping his head back, staggering, before he finally goes down.

BUDDY

I don't believe it.

Foley watches the new inmate as fights erupt all around him and, anxious now, he tries to get out of there.

EXT. PRISON YARD. DAY

Foley and Buddy sit atop a cement picnic table watching as, nearby, the 'winning' boxer – still wearing last night's pummelling on his face – gloats to a group of cons. He throws a fake punch at one of them as he demonstrates his winning technique.

BUDDY

Guy's braggin' he won a thrown fight. Fuckin' pathetic.

Foley looks at the other side of the yard, where Maurice now stands at the far side, coldly watching the guy, one hand thrust into his pocket. Foley watches as Maurice stops the new inmate – the older guy who looked out of place at the fight – as he comes out into the yard.

FOLEY

It's Richard Ripley.

BUDDY

(*looking now*)

The Wall Street guy? Oh, yeah. I didn't recognize him without his rug.

Foley watches as Maurice talks to the new inmate, the guy nodding, acquiescent, respectful.

FOLEY

Dick the Ripper they called him, on account of all the people he ripped off.

Foley watches as Ripley now makes a note in a black book.

BUDDY

What's he doin' here?

GLENN

(*off-screen*)

Three years.

They look to where Glenn Michaels, the blond guy in dark shades we saw in Maurice's corner, works out on the bench press a few feet away. He's shirtless, tanned, in shape.

He got three years and fined fifty million dollars and wrote 'em a fucking cheque. Like that, fifty mil, signed his name.
(*struggles with the bar*)
Whoa – little help here!

FOLEY

Who you talkin' to, Studs? Me, or Buddy. I can't tell, you got those shades on.

GLENN

You guys – come on – this is too heavy!

FOLEY

I guess the bright glare out here made it hard to see the numbers on the weights.

GLENN

I'll take the shades off. Just get this fuckin' thing off me.

Foley helps him get the bar up. Glenn sits up.

BUDDY

How do you know he wrote a cheque?

GLENN

He told me. He works the laundry with me. The guy loves to talk.

FOLEY

Yeah, to the US Attorney. I hear he rolled over on all the snitches he was doing business with and got 'em all brought up.

He watches Snoopy talking to Ripley, one eye always on the swaggering boxer across the yard, one hand in his pocket.

GLENN

Hey, anybody that can write a cheque for fifty mil, he says

*any*thing, I'm all fucking ears. Like the other day, he tells me how he's got all this money in foreign banks, plus around five mil in uncut diamonds at his house. He said, quote, 'Where I can put my hands on it anytime.'

BUDDY

Cool. Where's the guy live?

Foley watches a few more of Maurice's friends surround Ripley. Again, Ripley takes out his black book, starts nodding, making notations.

GLENN

Detroit. Snoopy Miller told me uncut diamonds are as easy to move as cash.

FOLEY

Ever seen an uncut diamond, Studs? They look like plain old rocks.

GLENN

So. What's your point?

FOLEY

My point is, that's probably what you're gonna end up with.

GLENN

You think he's lying?

FOLEY

Use your head. The guys got five million lying around his house, you really think he's gonna tell some motormouth he just met in prison about it?

A bell sounds. Everyone starts walking for the gate.

Foley watches as the boxer and his crew head for the gate, Maurice still standing there with his hand in his pocket.

Slow motion as the boxer gets to the gate, sees Maurice, who moves to him now, smiling like he's so glad to see him . . . his left hand clapping the guy on the back, saying something like 'congratulations' as now his right hand comes out of his pocket and we see the long metal shiv –

BUDDY
(*watching Snoopy*)

Here it comes.

Maurice wraps his left arm around the boxer's shoulder and hugs him tight for a moment, then quickly moves away. The boxer stands there like a statue, doesn't move until he's at last jostled from behind and his legs fold and he drops to the cement.

I guess the Snoop doesn't like to lose, even if it's on purpose.

We hear a whistle blow as a guard spots the body. And now everyone moves like hell for the gate . . . except for . . .

Richard Ripley, who stands there frozen, staring down at the body.

Foley glances back at the approaching guards, casually takes Ripley by the arm as he passes, leads him away from there, talks to him as they walk into the block . . .

FOLEY

You don't wanna be standing there, the hacks start asking questions you don't wanna answer.

RIPLEY

Oh, uh, right, thanks . . .

Foley then moves away. He sees Maurice looking back at him, giving him a hard stare just before he melts into the crowd.

DISSOLVE TO:

INT. FOLEY'S CELL. BELLE GLADE. DAY (NOW)

He lies there another moment when . . .

. . . a pair of legs swings down over the side from the top bunk. Foley's cellmate jumps down, walks the three feet or so to the

toilet, casually pulls down his pants and starts to go to the bathroom. Foley shakes his head and turns away.

EXT. STRIP MALL. DAY

Buddy walks up to a Cadillac Sedan DeVille Concours pulling a slim-jim from the back of his pants, about to jimmy the door, when he sees . . .

. . . a woman – middle-aged, wearing pearls and high heels – come out of the Winn Dixie pushing a grocery cart full of groceries.

Buddy sticks the jimmy back in his pants, waits until the woman is opening her trunk before coming forward.

BUDDY

Here, lemme help you with those, ma'am.

She doesn't seem too sure about it, but lets him load the groceries in the trunk and take the key out of the lock.

WOMAN

I didn't ask for your help, so don't expect a tip.

Buddy smiles, waves her off.

BUDDY

That's OK, ma'am. I'll just take your car.

She stands there stupidly as he gets in and drives off.

INT. CHAPEL. DUSK

In the midst of a remodel. As door opens and Pup comes in, Foley puts a finger to his lips.

FOLEY

They're right underneath you, Pup. They dug a tunnel.

Foley watches Pup creep up the aisle towards the front of the chapel, eyes on the floor, listening . . .

PUP

I don't hear 'em. Where's the tunnel come out?

Pup turns his back, walks up the aisle and across the front of the pews to a window.

FOLEY

Second fence post from the tower out there. Go on, take a look.

As Pup stares out the window . . .

PUP

I don't see nothing there.

Foley reaches down into a pew where's stashed a four-foot crucifix. He picks it up, starts up the aisle . . .

FOLEY

You will directly. Keep watching.

INT. KAREN SISCO'S CAR. DUSK

The high beams from her car show the prison parking area, then the fence strung with razor wire. Karen parks near the fence, lights a cigarette and dials her car phone.

KAREN

Hi. Karen Sisco again for Ray Nicolet.

(*beat*)

He's not? Could you tell him that . . . never mind. I'll call back.

Headlights hit Karen's rear-view mirror, a car pulling in behind her. The lights go off, then come on again. She adjusts the mirror to deflect the glare.

INT. THE CAR BEHIND HER. DUSK

Buddy sits watching the cons come in from the athletic field. He sees the mirror flash in the car in front of him as Karen checks her face out in the rear-view.

INT. CHAPEL. DUSK

As Foley moves up behind Pup, he lets his jacket fall to the floor, holds the crucifix down against his leg.

PUP

There some car headlights out there . . .

(*then*)

Jesus Christ . . .

Now he pulls his radio from his belt, says into it . . .

Man outside the fence! By tower six!

(*responds to radio*)

This is Officer Pupko . . .

(*then*)

I'm looking at him, for Christ's sake!

OK – *now Foley raises the metal cross, steps in and lays it smack against the side of Pup's head. Drops him clean with one swing, bouncing him off the window frame and down without a sound coming from him.*

INT. KAREN SISCO'S CAR. DUSK

As Karen grabs the court papers off the seat, she opens her car door, glances at the fence and pauses as she sees a figure there, crouching down.

Karen turns on her headlights. No, *not crouched. The guy is* coming out of the ground. *On* this *side of the fence.*

Head and shoulders appear and another guy comes out of the ground. Right in front of her.

Karen leans on the horn, holds it down and sees the two guys by the fence – Chino and Lulu – look into her headlights, poised there for a moment before taking off into the dark. Karen gets out of the car.

INT. BUDDY'S CAR. DUSK

As Buddy watches a spotlight from the tower come on and follow the two cons, we then hear the sound of rifle reports before the men disappear into the dark.

Then Buddy sees Karen in his headlights, whistles softly as he gets a good look at her long legs as she raises the lid to her trunk . . .

BUDDY

What's she doing?

He watches her duck her head in the trunk and come out with a holstered pistol.

Uh-oh.

But then she throws the pistol in the trunk, ducks in there again and comes out this time racking a shotgun.

Uh-oh.

And now Buddy watches her hurry to the front of her car and raise the shotgun as we hear a whistle blow in the compound. Buddy gets out of the car.

EXT. PARKING AREA. DUSK

Karen puts the shotgun on two more cons, both filthy dirty, standing by the hole they just crawled out of.

KAREN

Get your hands in the air!

Buddy watches the two cons, both Latins, make up their minds, start edging away – shit, they've come this far.

They look out at the spotlight sweeping around in the dark, then look the other way, along the fence towards the main gate, to see armed hacks coming out on the run, and that decides it for the cons. They take off running.

Now Buddy watches as Karen puts her pump gun on them, but doesn't fire.

The hacks running from the gate with rifles beat her to it, open all at once and keep firing until the two convicts are cut down as they run.

The hacks glance at Karen, but don't bother with her, more interested in the hole the convicts had come out of. Now they're standing by it peering in, edging closer with their weapons ready; then they step back at once, bump into each other as . . .

A head appears wearing a guard's baseball cap, the guy now saying something to the guards, his face smeared with muck, excited, pointing towards the orange grove.

They run off, pausing briefly to kick the convicts they shot to see if they're alive, then keep going.

The man in the hole, Foley, climbs out. He takes his time, puts on a show, standing with his hands on his hips like an honest-to-God hack, that serious cap down on his eyes.

Buddy waves to Foley to come on and Karen turns and puts the shotgun on Buddy. Buddy raises the palm of his hand.

BUDDY

It's OK, honey, we're good guys.

KAREN

What're you doing here?

Not so much asking, but putting it to him the way cops do when they're already pretty sure what you're doing. She glances around to include Foley, now coming at her like some creature out of the swamp, giving Buddy time to take her around the neck.

She fights him, jabs him in the gut with the butt end of the shotgun before Foley wrenches it from her grip.

They drag her to the rear end of her car, the trunk lid still up, and crouch there as some hacks come running along the fence, past the dark gun tower and cross the road towards the orange grove. A moment later, they hear bursts of gunfire, then silence.

FOLEY

I bet that's all the hacks they send out. Otherwise nobody's left to mind the store.

BUDDY

Why don't we talk about it later?

He turns to see Foley and Karen staring at each other in the headlights from Buddy's car; Karen not at all afraid.

FOLEY

Why, you're just a girl. What do you do for a living you pack a shotgun?

KAREN

I'm a federal marshal and you're under arrest, both of you guys.

Foley keeps staring at her like he's giving the situation serious thought, but what he says is . . .

FOLEY

I bet I smell, don't I?

(*pause*)

Listen, you hop in the trunk and we'll get out of here.

Karen looks at him, then gets up, climbs into the trunk. She's reaching around, trying to find her pistol, when . . .

Foley gives her a shove and gets in with her, wedging her against the wall of the trunk, pressing against her back like they're cuddled up in bed.

He holds her to him, giving her no room to turn and stick the gun in his face. Buddy reaches for the trunk lid and then everything goes . . .

BLACK

Total darkness, not a crack or a pinpoint of light showing. Then we hear the engine come to life, the car moving along.

FOLEY

(*voice-over*)

You comfy?

KAREN

(*voice-over*)

If I could have a little more room.

FOLEY

(*voice-over*)

There isn't any. All this shit you got in here. What is all this stuff anyway? Handcuffs, chains . . . what's this can?

KAREN

(*voice-over*)

For your breath. You could use it. Squirt some in your mouth.

FOLEY

(*voice-over*)

You devil, it's mace, huh? What've you got here, a billy? Use it on poor unfortunate offenders.

A beam of light appears as he finds a flashlight and turns it on. He plays the beam along Karen's leg, calms down some as he looks at all of her now and finally says . . .

Where's your gun, your pistol?

KAREN

In my bag, in the car.

They go over some bumps. We hear men's voices from somewhere far off, outside.

You know you don't have a chance of making it. Guards are out here already, they'll stop the car.

He runs his hand down her thigh, looking for her gun, but also, just, well, looking.

FOLEY

They're off in the cane by now chasing Cubans. I timed it to slip between the cracks, you might say.

EXT. CAR. NIGHT

Buddy floors it away from the prison, checks the rear-view mirror.

INT. TRUNK. NIGHT

Foley tries to wipe some of the mud off his face.

FOLEY

Boy, it stunk in there.

KAREN

I believe it. You've ruined a nine-hundred-dollar suit my dad gave me.

FOLEY

Yeah, went real nice with that twelve-gauge, too.

(*pause*)

Tell me, why in the world would someone like you ever become a federal marshal?

KAREN

The idea of going after guys like you appealed to me.

FOLEY

Guys like me, huh. Well, listen, even though I've been celibate lately, I'm not gonna force myself on you. I've never done that in my life.

KAREN

You wouldn't have time anyway. We come to a roadblock, they'll run the car, find out in five seconds who it belongs to.

FOLEY

If they get set up in time, which I doubt. And even if they do they'll be looking for a buncha little Latin fellas, not a big black guy driving a Ford.

KAREN

Must be quite a pal, risk his own ass like this.

More bumps. Then picking up speed as the road smooths out.

FOLEY

Who, Buddy? Yeah. He's a good guy. Back when we jailed together, he'd call his sister every week without fail. She's a born-again Christian, does book-keeping for a televangelist. Buddy calls her up, confesses his sins, tells her about whatever bank he happened to rob.

KAREN

Buddy. That's his given name?

FOLEY

(*whoops, beat*)

One I gave him, yeah.

(*mouths*)

Fuck . . .

INT. CAR. NIGHT

Buddy rifles through Karen's bag while he drives. He looks up from her badge and ID case at the road.

INT. TRUNK. NIGHT

KAREN

So, what's *your* name? It'll be in the paper tomorrow anyway.

FOLEY

Jack Foley. You've probably heard of me.

KAREN

Why, are you famous?

FOLEY

Time I was convicted in California? FBI told me I'd robbed more banks than anyone in the computer.

KAREN

How many was that?

FOLEY

Tell you the truth, I don't know. I started when I was eighteen, driving for my Uncle Cully and his partner, Gus. They go into a bank this one time in Slidell, Gus jumps the counter to get to the tellers and breaks his leg. All three of us ended up in Angola.

KAREN

That's funny.

FOLEY

I thought so, too.

KAREN

It was me, I woulda left ol' Gus on the floor.

FOLEY

I believe you would have. Another fall, I did seven years at Lompoc. And I don't mean the place next door where some of Nixon's people went.

KAREN

I know the difference. You were in Lompoc USP, the federal penitentiary. I've delivered people there. So basically you've spent half your life in prison.

FOLEY

(*beat*)

Basically. Yeah. If I go back now, I do a full thirty years, no time off. Can you imagine looking at that?

KAREN

I don't have to. I don't rob banks.

He looks at her, then looks away.

EXT. CAR. NIGHT

The car turns into a main highway.

INT. TRUNK. NIGHT

Foley plays the light down the length of her.

FOLEY

You don't seem all that scared.

KAREN

Of course I am.

FOLEY

You don't act like it.

KAREN

What do you want me to do? Scream? I don't think it would help much.

(*pause*)

I'm just gonna sit back, take it easy, and wait for you to screw up.

FOLEY

Jesus, you sound like my ex-wife.

KAREN

You were married? All those falls, I'm surprised you had time.

FOLEY

It was just a year, give or take a few days. I mean, it's not like we didn't get along or anything. We had fun, we just didn't have that . . . that thing, you know? That spark, you know what I mean? You gotta have that.

KAREN
(*thinking*)

Uh-huh.

FOLEY

We still talk, though.

KAREN

Sure.

EXT. CAR. NIGHT

Buddy passes a sign that says 'MIAMI, 74 MILES'.

INT. TRUNK. NIGHT

Karen tries to get a look at Foley.

KAREN

You know, this isn't gonna end well, these thing never do.

FOLEY

Yeah, well, if it turns out I get shot like a dog, it'll be in the street, not off a goddamn fence.

KAREN

You must see yourself as some kind of Clyde Barrow.

And for a few moments, all we hear is the sound of the car on the road. Then . . .

FOLEY

Oh, you mean of Bonnie and Clyde? Hm. You ever see pictures of him, the way he wore his hat? You could tell he had that don't-give-a-shit air about him.

KAREN

I don't recall his hat, but I've seen pictures of him lying dead, shot by Texas Rangers. Did you know he didn't have his shoes on?

FOLEY

Is that right?

KAREN

They put a hundred-and-eighty-seven bullet holes in Clyde, Bonnie Parker and the car they were driving. Bonnie was eating a sandwich.

FOLEY

You're full of interesting facts, aren't you?

KAREN

It was May 1934, near Gibsland, Louisiana.

EXT. HIGHWAY. NIGHT

Quiet. Empty. A moment later a car flies past.

INT. TRUNK. NIGHT

FOLEY

That part in the movie where they get shot? Warren Beatty and . . . I can't think of her name.

KAREN

Faye Dunaway.

FOLEY

Yeah, I liked her in that movie about TV . . .

KAREN

Network. Yeah, she was good.

FOLEY

And the guy saying he wasn't gonna take any more shit from anybody . . .

KAREN

Peter Finch.

FOLEY

Yeah, right. Anyway, that scene where Warren Beatty and Faye Dunaway get shot? I remember thinking at the time it wouldn't be a bad way to go, if you have to.

KAREN

Bleeding on a country road.

FOLEY

It wasn't pretty after, no, but if you were in that car – eating a sandwich – you wouldn't have known what hit you.

We hear faint sirens off-screen . . .

INT. CAR. NIGHT

Buddy sees flashing lights approach from the opposite direction. He stays cool as the green-and-whites get closer . . . closer . . . then fly right on past.

INT. TRUNK. NIGHT

The sirens scream at us for a moment, then fade.

FOLEY

You're sure easy to talk to. I wonder – say we met under different circumstances and got to talking, say you were in a bar and I came up to you – I wonder what would happen.

KAREN

Nothing.

FOLEY

I mean if you didn't know who I was.

KAREN

You'd probably tell me.

FOLEY

I'm just saying I think if we met under different circumstances . . .

KAREN

You have to be kidding.

Silence. Foley tries to get back to where it was working . . .

FOLEY

Another one Faye Dunaway was in I liked, *Three Days of the Condor.*

KAREN

With Robert Redford, when he was young.

FOLEY

Yeah . . .

They lie there a moment, thinking about that, as we hear the car slowing down, coasting, then bumping along the shoulder of the road to a stop.

KAREN

I never thought it made sense, though, the way they got together so quick.

FOLEY

Really.

KAREN

I mean, romantically.

FOLEY

Uh-huh.

(*pause*)

Well, but if –

The trunk goes dark again as the car's turned off.

BUDDY

(*off-screen*)

You still alive in there?

And the trunk lid raises so that we see Karen and Foley lying in the back. Foley gets out. Karen doesn't move.

FOLEY

(*off-screen*)

Where in the hell are we?

BUDDY

That's the turnpike up there. Glenn's waiting with the other car.

FOLEY

OK, honey, come on out of there.

Karen pushes off, rolls from her right side to her left, brings up her Sig-Sauer in both hands to put it on them, both standing in the opening, in the dark, but right there.

KAREN

Get your hands up and turn around. *Now.*

FOLEY

Shit . . .

Foley brings the lid down, he and Buddy moving in opposite directions as she begins firing from the inside . . .

Buddy and Foley hook up again in front of the car. We can see they're beneath an overpass. Foley stares at the trunk.

BUDDY

We may as well leave her. We're leaving the car and we gotta leave her some place anyway. What's the difference where?

FOLEY

She's coming with us.

Foley walks to the passenger seat, reaches in the window.

BUDDY

Jesus Christ, what were you doing in there?

FOLEY

Get the shotgun. And her purse. I'd like to know who she is.

Foley takes her wallet, looks at her driver's licence photo.

BUDDY

I already looked. Her name is Karen Sisco. Like the Cisco Kid only spelled different, S-i-s-c-o.

A sheriff's green-and-white goes screaming past and they keep to the narrow space between the car and the concrete abutment of the overpass. When the road quietens down, Foley moves to the trunk and bangs on it once with his fist.

FOLEY

Karen? Be a good girl now, you hear? Now, I'm gonna open the –

Foley jumps at the sound of a pistol shot.

You're putting holes in your car!

He looks up to see Buddy holding her shotgun, staring at him. He settles down, then . . .

We're not leaving you. I'm gonna open the trunk enough for you to throw the gun out. OK? You shoot – Buddy's got your shotgun, says he'll shoot back if you do and I can't stop him. So it's up to you.

Foley puts his hand out and Buddy, still looking at him funny, gives him the keys.

VOICE

Hey!

Coming from somewhere above them.

It's me, Glenn.

Foley steps out into the open, Buddy close behind him. They look up to see a figure, head and shoulders against the evening sky, leaning on the concrete overpass rail. We can see his long blond hair falling beside his face, now half-concealed behind dark sunglasses.

GLENN

Hey, Jack, good to see you, man. The fuck're you guys shooting at?

Foley looks at Buddy.

FOLEY

Do we need him?

BUDDY

The green-and-whites saw us. One of 'em starts thinking, what's that car doing there? Ties it to the break and turns around . . .

Foley thinks about it, then looks up at the overpass again.

FOLEY

Oh, hey, Studs? We thought you were somebody else.

GLENN

Studs. Man, I haven't heard that since Lompoc. What's going on?

FOLEY

Oh, nuthin'.

Foley shakes his head, then walks back to the Ford and bangs on the trunk.

You coming out?

Foley sticks the key in the lock as Buddy steps up to the trunk and racks the pump on the shotgun. Foley leans close to the metal.

You hear that?

He turns the key and raises the lid. Karen, bunched in there, extends her arm, her hand holding the Sig-Sauer by the barrel.

KAREN

You win, Jack.

'Jack.' Buddy gives him another funny look.

EXT. TOP OF OVERPASS. NIGHT

Glenn removes a note stuck in the side window of a stolen Audi that reads 'GONE TO GET GAS'.

FOLEY

(*off-screen*)

Have your clothes cleaned and send me the bill.

Glenn looks over as the three of them reach the top of the slope and move through the scrub. Glenn leans against the car, flashers blinking.

KAREN

I'll sent it to you at Glades.

GLENN

Jesus, what'd you crawl through, a sewer?

FOLEY

Take your sunglasses off.

GLENN

I see better with them on.

FOLEY

You don't take 'em off, I'm gonna throw 'em off the overpass while they're still on your head.

Glenn shrugs, takes them off and sticks them in his jeans.

Wait in the car.

GLENN

You're in civilization now, man, ease up.

FOLEY

I'd like you to go wait in the car. How's that? Take her with you and put her in back.

GLENN

In the trunk?

FOLEY

The back seat.

Foley stares at him, waiting. Glenn motions to Karen.

GLENN

Come on. I have to do what I'm told.

She walks past Foley without looking at him.

FOLEY

Wait a minute. Let me have your raincoat.
(*looks at Buddy*)
Somebody forgot to bring me clean clothes.

BUDDY

I brought 'em, they're back at Glades in the Cadillac. You wanted to take her car.

KAREN

You can blame me if you want. I don't mind.

He doesn't say anything as Glenn takes off the raincoat, folds it up, then throws it at Foley's feet.

GLENN

Here you are, sir.

Foley watches as Glenn gets his sunglasses out, puts them back on and takes Karen by the arm.

BUDDY

What's wrong with you?

Karen looks over at Foley, then ducks her head and gets in the back seat.

FOLEY

Why you brought Glenn into this, I'll never know.

BUDDY

How 'bout the score was his idea to begin with?

FOLEY

His idea? Gimme a break. Fuckin' guy's got a vacant lot for a head. Was you and me figured the whole thing out.

Buddy watches Foley struggle with the buttons on the uniform, all of them caked with muck.

BUDDY

You're pulling at it. Here . . .

He lays the shotgun in the grass and comes up, takes the guard shirt in his two hands and rips it open, popping buttons and tearing the shirt.

FOLEY

I don't know why, but every time he opens his mouth I want to punch him out.

BUDDY

He ain't the problem, Jack.

Foley looks at him.

You wanna pull your head outta your ass and tell me why we're bringing *her* with us?

INT. CAR. NIGHT

Karen watches Glenn get into the car, sees him as the dome light comes on for a second or two before he closes the door. He half-turns, laying his arm along the top of the seats, runs his hand through his hair . . .

GLENN

. . . if he thinks he can talk to me like this. Shit, I don't even know what I need them for.

Karen leans forward to have a look. Sees Foley and Buddy against the dark foliage.

I got a big score lined up up north. They wouldn't even know about it, it wasn't for me. I could do it right now myself, except it's so fucking cold up there in January –

KAREN

Glenn?

His head turns so that we can see his designer shades.

You don't remember me, do you?

GLENN

(*beat*)

It couldn't have been out at Glades, if that's what you're thinking. I was never out there.

KAREN

No, that's not what I'm thinking.

He raises his hand, strokes his hair away from his face.

GLENN

But you're sure we've met, huh?

KAREN

Last fall, I drove you from the Palm Beach county jail to the federal courthouse, twice. You're Glenn Michaels.

(*pause*)

I never forget anyone I've cuffed and shackled.

He doesn't move or say a word, staring at her now like he's been turned to stone.

Let's think for a minute, Glenn, see if we can work this out . . .

He turns away, all the way around to look straight ahead.

Do we have a gun in the car?

GLENN

I remember you now. Shit.

KAREN

Foley's not going to make it. And if he goes down, Glenn, you go with him.

She touches his shoulder and he jumps.

Look, I can understand if you and Foley are close.

GLENN

We're not. I'm helping him, yeah –

KAREN

Wait. *Have* you helped him, Glenn? At this point, technically, I doubt you could be charged with aiding a fugitive. So you still have a choice. You can help him and risk going down again, get cuffed and shackled, hope to God you pull a reasonable judge, not some hard-on. Or, if you want to play it another way . . .

She pauses. He turns and looks at her.

GLENN

Like how?

EXT. OVERPASS. NIGHT

Foley watches a car pass on the highway.

BUDDY

You want to take her to my place and get cleaned up? You come out of the bathroom with your aftershave on and she goes, 'Oh, I had you all wrong'?

FOLEY

I want to talk to her again, that's all. See what would happen under, you know, normal circumstances.

BUDDY

You're too late, Jack.

Foley doesn't say anything. Just takes a deep breath as we hear the car start and they both look over.

He wants to get out of here and I don't blame him.

They start towards the car. Then stop and watch as it takes off, tyres squealing as the rubber hits pavement. Their backs to us, they stand there watching the taillights until they're out of sight down the turnpike, neither of them saying a word.

We hear squeaky footsteps over . . .

CUT TO:

A CORRIDOR IN LOMPOC FPC

As Maurice Miller and his 'man' – a big black bulk named Himey – strut purposefully up the hall.

They step into the prison library, where Richard Ripley sits at one of the tables reading a big coffee-table book called The Warm World of Tropical Fish.

MAURICE

Dick. My man.

Ripley looks up as Maurice and Himey come strolling into the library and sit down on either side of a now very anxious Ripley.

I got your fishies for you.

He sets a small Ziploc with two tiny fish inside down on the table.

RIPLEY

(*reaches for them*)

Thank you . . .

MAURICE

(*pulls them back*)

Not so fast, Dick.

(*off Ripley's look*)

Starting now, there's gonna be an across the board cost a living increase.

RIPLEY

What?

MAURICE

Year ago, I come in here on credit card fraud, but after I shanked that loudmouth pussy on the yard the other day, my Dunn & Broadstreet has gone way the fuck up.

RIPLEY

I think it's Dunn & *Brad*street. But then, I could be wrong . . .

MAURICE

Whoever. The point is, prices are goin' up, too. Better get your little black book out, Richard. We got some business to talk about.

Ripley sighs, takes out his black book and opens it.

Let's start with the fish. They was two grand, but now they's three.

Ripley looks at the two tiny fish in the bag.

That Bausch & Lomb Saline shit you asked for is gonna be eighty bucks.

RIPLEY

(*writing*)

Well, I need that . . .

MAURICE

. . . and that extra pillow's gonna be an even three Cs.

VOICE

Hey.

They all look to where . . .

Jack Foley sits at the far end of the table, reading a thick manual of some kind. Himey gives him a mean stare. Foley points to a sign that says 'QUIET PLEASE'.

FOLEY

Sign says 'Shut the fuck up.' Or can't you guys read?

MAURICE

(*beat*)

There a problem, Foley?

FOLEY

Yeah.

Foley shuts the big book – Chilton's Auto Repair.

FOLEY

Yeah, I got a problem. This is the dumbest fucking shakedown in the history of dump shakedowns. Three hundred bucks for a pillow?

MAURICE

That's right.

RIPLEY

Sounds high, doesn't it?

FOLEY

Must be a real soft pillow.

MAURICE

Faux goose down.

RIPLEY

Still . . .

FOLEY

How much for your company at chow?

MAURICE

Company, shit. I watch the man's back.

FOLEY

I bet. How much?

MAURICE

Another C.

Foley shakes his head, turns to Ripley.

FOLEY

You're smart, Ripley, you'll tell this guy to fuck off.

RIPLEY

Really? Well, I uhhh . . .

FOLEY

First of all, if he kills you, he's not gonna get any more money out of you.

Ripley looks at Maurice: good point.

MAURICE

Man doesn't have to get killed. He could accidentally fall on something sharp, like a shiv. Or a dick.

Ripley turns back to Foley now: also a good point.

FOLEY

You stick *anything* in this guy, Snoop, they transfer his ass outta here faster'n you can throw a fight, and you still end up with nothing.

Ripley nods, takes this in.

MAURICE

This doesn't concern you, Foley. Why don't you go on out to the yard, have yourself a smoke?

FOLEY

I don't smoke.

HIMEY

(*slowly rising*)

You heard the man. Go on outta here.

Foley doesn't move, just gives the guy a bored once-over.

MAURICE

Himey here's a pro-toh-jay of mine. He's ranked number thirty-two in the federal prison system.

FOLEY

(*looking at Himey*)

Thirty-two outta what, twenty?

Himey bulldozes forward, pulling his massive fist back to clock Foley in the head when . . .

In one swift motion Foley brings his book up in one hand, like he's throwing a pie, and drives the hefty repair manual into Himey's face, snapping the big guy's head back, sending his feet flying out from under him so that he hits the floor back-first with a loud thud.

Maurice goes for Foley, who picks up the chair just as we hear a whistle. They all freeze and look to a prisoner at another table, who nods towards the door.

We pan over just as a guard appears, takes in the scene as a dazed Himey slowly pulls himself up, covers his now bleeding nose.

GUARD

What's going on here?

MAURICE

Oh, you know, reading's funnamental an' shit, we just excited.

GUARD

Clear outta here.

The guard exits. Maurice and Foley are still staring at each other.

RIPLEY

Excuse me. Snoopy? Did we settle the fish thing?

MAURICE

(*looks at Foley*)

Yeah. Sure. It's all settled.

He pours the water out of the bag and drops the fish into Ripley's open hand. Maurice then squeezes Ripley's hand into a fist, crushing the fish. He taps his fist to Ripley's.

RIPLEY

That's how you do it.

Maurice gives Foley a last look, starts out of the room with Himey. Ripley looks at the crushed fish in his hand, then at Foley.

RIPLEY

Thanks for your help.

FOLEY

Any time.

We hear a phone ring and then . . .

CUT TO:

MAURICE MILLER'S HOUSE. THE BEDROOM (NOW)

Maurice lies in bed watching a boxing match on television.

MAURICE

Stick and jab, fool. Stick and jab.

A frisbee whizzes past the television. We hear a dog yelp off-screen.

Hey! Watch that shit!

Maurice's girlfriend, Moselle – about thirty, sleepy-eyed, in a green bathrobe – picks the frisbee up off the floor as the phone rings away on the bedside table right next to Maurice.

MOSELLE

(*calls off-screen*)

Tuffy. C'mere, boy . . .

MAURICE

You gonna answer the phone?

MOSELLE

What for? It's not for me.

Maurice watches as Moselle now tries to throw the frisbee to a little wire-haired terrier, but it just bounces off the dog's head.

Bad dog.

MAURICE

(*scoops up the dog*)

Moselle, the fuck are you doing to my little Tuffy?

He lovingly nuzzles the dog like it's his child.

MOSELLE

I'm trainin' Tuffy, so he can be on a Kal Kan commercial, make us some extra money.

He looks at her.

MAURICE

That's the dumbest thing I heard in my life. Everybody knows Kal Kan doesn't pay for shit. You gonna get a gig, it's gotta be for one of the big three: Science Diet, Iams or that Cycle shit for the fat dogs. Now answer the fuckin' phone.

She comes over, picks up the phone.

MOSELLE

Hello?

(*hands it to Maurice*)

For you.

MAURICE

(*takes it*)

This is me.

EXT. PHONE BOOTH. GAS STATION. NIGHT

An antsy Glenn with his shades on talks on the phone.

GLENN

Snoopy. Glenn Michaels.

Intercutting Glenn and Maurice:

MAURICE

Studs. Hey, son, you must be one a them psychic friends. I was just thinkin' about you.

Glenn watches as some guy in a suit gets out of a black Lincoln Town Car and jogs to the john.

GLENN

Listen, Snoopy, I'm on my way up to Detroit and need a place to crash.

MAURICE

You crazy, come up *here*? It's fuckin' one degree outside.

GLENN

I wanna talk to you about a job.

MAURICE

Uh-huh.

GLENN

I can't really go into it right now. I'll just tell you it's someone big.

MAURICE

Some*one*? Gimme a hint.

GLENN

It's a guy you know.

MAURICE

Gimme another hint.

GLENN

It's Richard Ripley.

Maurice doesn't say a word.

You there?

MAURICE

Oh, I'm here, all right. I'm very here. Question is, why aren't *you* here?

EXT. BUDDY'S APARTMENT. SOMEWHERE IN FLORIDA. NIGHT

As Foley and Buddy hurry up the front steps.

FOLEY

I'm just saying she wasn't scared.

BUDDY

'Cause she had her hand on her gun the whole time, waiting to make her move.

Buddy opens the door, looks at Foley.

FOLEY

You're just jealous it was me in the trunk with her and not you.

BUDDY

You're right.

INT. BUDDY'S APARTMENT. NIGHT

A 'hideout'. Not much in the way of furnishings. Foley follows Buddy inside, watches as he bolts the door.

FOLEY

First thing I'm gonna do is get all this mud off me.

Foley starts for the bathroom.

I've been dreaming about a hot bath for the last six months. Soak the prison off me.

BUDDY

There's some lilac oil, you want some, a vanilla candle under the sink.

FOLEY

Oh, man.

BUDDY

There's something about a nice hot bath, transforms a person. It's not just about opening up your pores, know what I mean? There's just something about the heat and the wet that's calming, you know? Settles me in a way that I really can't articulate.

FOLEY

I know exactly what you mean. It's just a feeling.

(*beat*)

You know, I could go for some wine tonight.

BUDDY

There's a store around the corner, I'll be right back.

FOLEY

Sounds great.

Foley goes into the bathroom. A moment later we hear the bath running.

INT. APARTMENT HALLWAY. DAY

As Buddy leaves the apartment, starts down the hall, Karen steps into frame, watches as he disappears down the stairs. Gun drawn, she then moves towards the apartment.

INT. BATHROOM. DAY

As Foley undresses, picks up a candle off the sink and smells it. He notices his nude image in the mirror and checks himself out.

INT. APARTMENT. DAY

As Karen slips the door. She looks around, hears the water running.

She racks the slide on her gun, snicks off the safety and starts for the bathroom. Suddenly, the water is turned off. She stops where she is. She then moves a careful step at a time towards the open doorway.

Gradually the tub comes into view, beginning with Foley's feet resting crossed on the other end, then the middle of the tub, then she's in the doorway, looking down at . . .

Foley, lying there in the tub, his eyes closed. Karen cuts her eyes down the length of him, taking a moment here to check him out, long enough for Foley to open his eyes and grab her hand, the one holding the gun.

FOLEY

Hey.

They look at each other a moment. He then pulls her down to him and kisses her. She kisses him back. He then pulls her into the tub with him as we now hear . . .

MARSHALL SISCO

(*voice-over*)

Karen . . .?

CUT TO:

Karen as she opens her eyes.

KAREN

What?

INT. HOSPITAL ROOM. DAY

Flowers everywhere. Karen – bruises on her face – lies in bed. Her father, Marshall, sits on the chair beside her.

MARSHALL

You were talking in your sleep.

KAREN
(*beat*)

What'd I say?

MARSHALL

'Hey, yourself.'

KAREN

Huh.

We hear a knock at the door. They look to where Special Agent Daniel Burdon – black, forties, expensive suit – stands in the doorway, file in one hand.

KAREN

Hello, Daniel.

BURDON
(*to Marshall*)

Daniel Burdon, FBI.

MARSHALL

Marshall Sisco. Karen's dad.

BURDON

You mind please waiting outside. We have some business to do here.

Marshall looks at him a moment. Then, to Karen . . .

MARSHALL

I need to go to the john anyway.

Burdon waits for Marshall to walk out, then sits down.

KAREN

I wanna be on the task force, Daniel.

BURDON

That's nice of you to offer, Karen, but I got all the help I can use right now. Instead, let's talk about how you got the bump on your head.

KAREN
(*indicates file*)
Isn't that my report you're holding on to?

BURDON
Yes, but I want to hear you tell it. Starting with when you tried to grab the wheel – where was this?

KAREN
Coming to the Okeechobee exit . . .

And now we see it . . .

IN THE CAR

Going over a hundred miles per hour, blowing past cars . . .

KAREN
Take the next exit.

GLENN
What am I supposed to do *now*?

KAREN
Glenn, take the exit.

GLENN
No way, man, no fuckin' way am I gonna turn myself in.

She reaches over and grabs the wheel.

The fuck are you doing?!

He hits the brakes. The car goes off the road, down the slope, the abutment coming right at us as we go back to . . .

THE HOSPITAL ROOM

Burdon sets the file down, sits back now.

KAREN
The next thing I knew, the paramedics were taking me out of the car.

Burdon looks at Karen a moment, then . . .

BURDON

There's a couple of points I keep wondering about to do with the two guys that grabbed you. Buddy, is it? And this fella Jack Foley. I swear the man must've robbed two hundred banks in his time.

KAREN

Really? Huh. He told me he didn't remember how many he robbed.

BURDON

You talked to him?

KAREN

In the trunk, yeah?

BURDON

What'd you talk about?

KAREN

Oh . . . different things, prison, movies.

BURDON

This fella holds you hostage, you talk about movies?

KAREN

It was an unusual experience.

BURDON

Foley made me think of that fella Carl Tillman, the one you were seeing, it turns out the same time he was doing banks. You recall that?

KAREN

When I was seeing Carl Tillman, I didn't know he robbed banks.

BURDON

Yeah, but I had enough reason to believe he did, and I told you. So you had to at least suspect him.

KAREN

And what happened to Carl?

BURDON

The time came, you shot him. But you didn't shoot Foley or the guy with him. They're unarmed, you had a shotgun and you let them throw you in the trunk. OK, now you got your Sig in your hand. You say in the report you couldn't turn around, he had you pinned down. But when the trunk opened, how come you didn't cap the two guys then?

KAREN

Is that what you would've done?

BURDON

You say in the report Glenn didn't have a gun, but you let him get away, too.

KAREN

Daniel, what do you work on most of the time, fraud? Go after crooked book-keepers.

BURDON

Karen, I've been with the Bureau fifteen years, on all kinds of investigations.

KAREN

Have you ever shot a man? How many times have you been primary through the door?

BURDON

I have to qualify, is that it?

KAREN

You have to know what you're talking about.

We hear chuckling off-screen. Burdon glances at the doorway, where we see Marshall now standing, enjoying this.

BURDON

We'll talk another time, Karen. All right? I'd like to know why

Foley put you in that second car when he didn't need you any more.

KAREN

You'll have to ask him.

BURDON

Sounds to me like he liked having you around. I'll see you, Karen. Mr Sisco.

MARSHALL

Agent Burdon.

Marshall waits for him to walk out.

The white man's Burdon. That's what everybody calls him in Miami. The Metro-Dade guys. He's got a knack for pissing people off.

She's not listening. He sits down, takes her hand.

What are you thinking about?

KAREN

The Sig-Sauer you got me for my birthday.

MARSHALL

Tell you what, you're a good girl, you might get another one for Christmas.

She looks at him.

KAREN

I'll get it back when I get Foley.

EXT. BUDDY'S APARTMENT BUILDING. DAY

A dozen geriatric residents sit on chairs out front as Buddy climbs the steps carrying a bag of groceries under one arm, newspaper under the other. An old woman comes out the door as Buddy opens it and squints at him.

OLD WOMAN

Oh – are you delivering the oxygen?

BUDDY

Uh, no, ma'am. Sorry.

INT. BUDDY'S APARTMENT. DAY

Buddy's real apartment, not the one Karen pictured in her dream. This one's nicer, with a view of the beach. Jack stands on the balcony going through Karen's bag.

He pulls out her wallet, checks out her driver's licence photo. He does the same with her gym ID card. He finds her address book and opens it up. A photo of her father slips out. Jack examines it a moment, then flips through the book.

He stares at something in her bag a moment, then reaches in and comes up with her US Marshal ID. He slips it open and studies the badge and the picture opposite.

He holds on to it, looks out at the ocean, but really sees . . .

THE OPEN TRUNK OF THE CAR – LAST NIGHT

As Karen gets out, saying . . .

KAREN

You win, Jack.

INT. BUDDY'S APARTMENT. DAY

Foley turns away from the view as Buddy walks in, sets the grocery bag down on the coffee table.

BUDDY

You made the front page.

He holds up the newspaper so that Foley can see his picture on the front page: an unflattering mug shot that doesn't look all that much like him.

They pass this picture around you can go anywhere you want, nobody'll know you.

FOLEY

I wasn't feeling my best that day. I'd just drawn thirty to life.

BUDDY

Maybe this'll make you feel better.

Buddy reaches into the bag, tosses Foley a new Zippo.

FOLEY

Thanks.

Foley catches the lighter, immediately begins playing with it. He looks at the paper on the coffee table as Buddy sits down, pulls some groceries and a six-pack from the bag.

BUDDY

Paper says there's ten grand each on you, Chino and Lulu.

FOLEY

Say anything in there about Karen Sisco?

BUDDY

Just that she got away.

FOLEY

Yeah, but what happened after she drove off with Glenn?

BUDDY

You'll have to ask Glenn. And most likely, he's on his way to Detroit, where we should be.

Foley walks back out on to the balcony, looks at the contents of Karen's bag spread out on the table.

You realize what you're doing? Worrying about a person that works in law enforcement. You want to sit down and have cocktails with a girl that tried to shoot you. You hear what I'm saying?

Foley holds up the picture of Marshall Sisco.

FOLEY

Think this old guy is her boyfriend? It's the only picture she carries.

BUDDY

Am I going to Detroit by myself?

Foley picks up her driver's licence photo.

Longer we hang around down here, Jack, better chance there is either Glenn's gonna fuck up the whole score, or we gonna get busted, or both.

FOLEY

We'll leave first thing in the morning.

EXT. MARSHALL SISCO'S CONDO. DAY

Right on a marina. Boats bobbing on the water.

MARSHALL

(*voice-over*)

Is *this* Foley?

INT. MARSHALL SISCO'S CONDO. DAY

Marshall sits in his chair holding up a newspaper as Karen hands him a drink. She stares at the photograph.

KAREN

He doesn't even look like that.

MARSHALL

No?

KAREN

No, he looks a lot . . .

She realizes Marshall's watching her.

Different.

The doorbell rings. She ignores his look, gets up. Walks to the door and opens it to reveal Ray Nicolet – boots, leather jacket, etc. Cowboy Cop.

Hi, Ray.

RAY

You look great. Your dad taking good care of you?

KAREN

He took the week off so we'd have time together. So far he's worked on his boat every day. Dad? Ray Nicolet.

Marshall gets up, shakes his head.

RAY

I've heard a lot about you, Mr Sisco.

MARSHALL

Likewise.

KAREN

Ray's with the FBI Task Force, working on the prison break.

MARSHALL

(*eyeing his T-shirt*)

I see that.

Ray turns to Karen, holding his jacket open to show the Task Force inscription on his T-shirt in red. The guy's .357 is tucked into his waistband.

In case no one knows what he does. Tell me, Ray, you ever wear one says, 'Undercover'?

RAY

No. 'Course not.

KAREN

(*changing the subject*)

How's it going?

RAY

Great. We got one of 'em.

Karen looks at him.

KAREN

Was it Foley?

MARSHALL

(*before he can answer*)

Off a tip?

RAY

Yeah, someone spotted two of 'em in this hobo camp out by the airport, called the number –

MARSHALL

I knew it, soon as I saw they were offering a reward.

She grabs Nicolet by the arm.

KAREN

Was it Foley?

Marshall looks at her.

RAY

Foley? Oh. No, it was one of the Cubans. Linares.

KAREN

Oh . . .

RAY

We went out there, full SWAT, two choppers, the whole bit, but Linares started shooting anyway. We put him down, but somehow Chirino got away.

MARSHALL

Did you pay the guy the reward?

RAY

Yeah, as soon as we got back.

KAREN

Foley hadn't been there?

Her father gives her a look.

RAY

This place was strictly Cuban. If Foley had a ride he must have his own agenda. He seems to be the only one knows what he's doing.

The phone rings. Marshall moves to it.

MARSHALL

Hello?

(*beat*)

Yeah, she is. Just a minute.

(*hands her the phone*)

For you.

KAREN

Hello?

CUT TO:

Foley on the phone. On the balcony. Flipping through a copy of Vogue *while Buddy watches television inside.*

FOLEY

Hi.

Intercutting Karen and Foley:

Karen just stands there, sees her father looking at her as Ray drones on.

You know who this is?

KAREN

Yes.

She walks out to her father's balcony now.

FOLEY

I just wanted to see if you're OK, make sure Glenn didn't hurt you or, you know, anything.

MARSHALL

Something I've been wondering, Ray . . .

Marshall picks up the newspaper . . .

It says in the headline, '"I slept with a murderer," says shaken Miami woman.' She lives in Little Havana, her husband's out of town working when one of the escapees shows up at her door.

She closes the glass door, so that they won't hear her.

KAREN

How'd you get this number?

FOLEY

Who was it answered the phone?

KAREN

None of your business.

FOLEY

I'm just worried maybe I'm not old enough for you.

KAREN

That's my dad.

FOLEY

Really. He has a cop's face.

KAREN

How do you know? Wait – you have my wallet.

FOLEY

And your gun.

KAREN

Think I could have them back?

FOLEY

How do we do that?

KAREN

Let's see. You could come on by my dad's place, drop 'em off.

FOLEY

Sure. I'll just leave 'em with the SWAT guy answers the door.

Foley stops flipping through the magazine, stares at what he's been looking for: an ad for Defiance perfume.

KAREN

There's a guy here on the Task Force right now. Maybe I should put him on the phone, let you two work it out.

FOLEY

You won't do that.

KAREN

Why not?

FOLEY

Because you're having too much fun.

She doesn't know what to say to that. Foley smells the ad.

Inside the house . . .

MARSHALL

. . . She fixes him pork chops and rice, the next thing you know they're making love on the sofa. She says he was very gentle.

RAY

I spoke to her. The guy told her he missed his little girl and she felt sorry for him.

MARSHALL

That's how you score now?

On the patio, Karen looks inside at her father talking with Ray Nicolet.

KAREN

My dad's retired. He was a private investigator. Forty years. I used to work for him.

FOLEY

I can just picture that, a cute girl like you following slip-and-fall and whiplash cheaters.

KAREN

Something I've been wondering, whatever happened to your Uncle Cully?

FOLEY

Why? You think he might tell you where I am?

KAREN

Unless you wanna tell me.

FOLEY

He's dead. He did twenty-seven years before he came out and died not too long after in Charity Hospital, I think trying to make up for all the good times he'd missed.

(*pause*)

That's not gonna be me.

KAREN

One last score, that the idea? Move to some island.

FOLEY

I'm partial to mountains myself. But if you like islands, we'll make it an island.

KAREN

Whatta you mean *we'll* make it an island?

FOLEY

I just thought maybe you and me could –

Buddy opens the door, sticks his head out, startles Foley.

BUDDY

Who you talking to?

KAREN

Is that Buddy?

Foley's caught off-guard, hangs up the phone. He looks at Buddy.

FOLEY

What?!

BUDDY

You better come see this.

INT. MARSHALL'S CONDO. DAY

Karen stands on the balcony another moment, then hangs up, opens the sliding door and walks back into the living room.

RAY

The woman also said he stole her husband's gun, a .22 pistol, and some of his clothes.

MARSHALL

So the woman's married. She goes to bed with this prison escapee because he misses his little girl and then tells the world about it. But you don't reveal her name, you protect her. It sounds like you're saying it's OK as long as her husband doesn't find out about it. Like the guy who cheats on his wife, saying what she doesn't know won't hurt her.

KAREN

Dad.

He looks over at her now. Gives her an innocent look.

MARSHALL

What?

INT. BUDDY'S APARTMENT. DAY

As Foley and Buddy watch a news report on the earlier events at the hobo camp. We catch a glimpse of Ray Nicolet, gun in his waistband, sticking his chest out for the camera.

Foley shakes his head as they show a shot of Lulu's body covered with a sheet.

FOLEY

Chino's gonna wanna talk to me.

BUDDY

He's running for his life, he doesn't give a shit about you.

FOLEY

He's gotta know by now that I gave him up back at Glades. He does, he's gonna try to find me. Maybe go see Adele, see what she knows.

BUDDY

He knows where she lives?

Foley doesn't answer. Buddy mutes the set. Turns to Foley.

Jack?

FOLEY

We were talking one time, drinking rum. I may've mentioned Adele, how she worked for a magician. Chino got interested. He's like, Yeah? How does he saw the woman in half? He wanted to meet her. Or get a look at her if she ever came to visit.

BUDDY

So call her up. Tell her don't talk to any Cubans.

FOLEY

Her phone's probably tapped.

BUDDY

And you know they're gonna have some people watching the hotel.

FOLEY

Shit.

EXT. MARSHALL SISCO'S BOAT. DAY

Karen stands there with her car keys and bag as Marshall paints the trim on the boat.

MARSHALL

Remember, pay attention to how she talks about Foley, her tone. Do it right, she'll tell you things she wouldn't tell Burdon. Tell her you think he's a nice guy. No, first tell her about being in the trunk with him, in the dark for half an hour, and see how she takes it. If she's in on it, what does she get for all the aggravation: cops breathing on her? I bet nothing. So she still likes him enough to stick her neck out. You think that's possible? What kind of guy is he?

KAREN

He's pretty laid-back, confident.

MARSHALL

He remind you of that guy, Tillman?

KAREN

Not at all.

MARSHALL

But you know he's dirty and you still wanna see him again.

KAREN

I want to bust his ass, put him in shackles.

MARSHALL

Maybe. But you're also curious about the man. Twice last night you asked your married boyfriend Nicolet about him. You were concerned, but you didn't want to show it.

KAREN

My married boyfriend – setting him up with that news story so you could talk about infidelity. I couldn't believe it.

MARSHALL

You like the wild ones, don't you? Tillman, Nicolet and now Foley. You know, I've always said there's a thin line between the cowboy cops and the armed robbers, all those guys that love to pack.

KAREN

Foley *kid*napped me.

MARSHALL

Yeah, but you talked all the way from GCI to the turnpike. It sounds more like a first date than a kidnapping.

She gives him a look. He goes back to his painting.

Go talk to the ex-wife.

INT. ADELE DELISI'S APARTMENT. DAY

Adele comes in, drops a stack of her cards on the glass-topped dining table and turns on the window air-conditioner when the phone rings. She grabs it.

ADELE

Hi, this is Adele speaking.

EXT. PAY PHONE. DAY

Adele's neighbourhood. Near the beach. Chino on the phone. He wears a painter's cap and a white jumpsuit.

CHINO

Oh, is this Adele?

ADELE
(*phone*)

Yes, it is.

CHINO

Uh – sorry. Wrong number.

He hangs up, glances about, then checks the little .22 stuck in one of his pockets. As he then starts off down the street, we can see the name 'COLOUR MY WORLD HOUSEPAINTING' *on the back of the jumpsuit.*

INT. BUDDY'S CAR. DAY

Buddy drives. Foley – in a bright orange and ochre beach outfit – is beside him. Buddy looks at him, shakes his head.

BUDDY

Nice disguise.

FOLEY

I'm a tourist.

BUDDY

You at least bring the gun?

FOLEY

(*lifts straw bag*)

In here with my suntan lotion and beach towel.

(*points*)

That's her place.

As they drive past, Buddy indicates a man on the steps out front, obviously FBI.

BUDDY

There. You see the guy sitting on the porch? The old ladies and one guy? You know they'll have a couple more in a car somewhere.

FOLEY

(*watching something else*)

Uh-huh . . .

Buddy follows Foley's gaze across the street.

A car door opens and Karen Sisco gets out, rifling in her bag for

change. She drops a quarter. Foley is now watching as she bends down to grab it, her skirt hiking way up her thigh.

BUDDY

Oh, my.

Foley watches, her hair in her face as she tries to reach under the car and grab it.

OK, you saw her. That's all you get.

They watch as she walks to the Normandie and shows the Young Agent her ID . . .

FOLEY

I guess Adele's in good hands.

BUDDY

Sure looks that way.

FOLEY

(*finally*)

Let's go to Detroit.

BUDDY

Now you're talkin'.

INT. HALLWAY OUTSIDE ADELE'S APARTMENT. DAY

Adele has the chain on the door, talks to Karen through the narrow opening.

ADELE

You were *both* in the trunk? Together?

KAREN

From Glades to the turnpike. Then I left with Glenn.

Karen watches Adele's face in the opening, freshly made-up, heavy on the eyeshadow and lip gloss.

The FBI didn't tell you I was with them?

ADELE

They didn't *tell* me anything, they asked questions.

KAREN

But you know what I'm talking about, don't you? About Glenn, don't you, and the second car?

ADELE

I know a Glenn.

She thinks a moment. The door closes and opens again, all the way. Adele stands there in a robe, hanging partly open, panties, but no bra.

I'm getting ready to go out. You can come in if you want, sit down for a minute. Would you like a Diet Coke?

KAREN

No, thanks.

She comes in, checks out the place. She turns a chair from the glass-top table and sits down as Adele comes out of the kitchenette with a Diet Coke and packet of cigarettes.

ADELE

Those are cute shoes. The kind of jobs I get, I have to wear these killer spikes, they ruin your feet.

She walks away, comes back with an ashtray.

When you were in the trunk with Jack . . .

Karen waits, watches her light her cigarette.

He didn't hurt you or anything, did he?

KAREN

You mean, did he try to jump me? No, but he was kind of talkative.

ADELE

He gets that way when he's nervous sometimes.

Adele sits down at the other end of the table.

KAREN

You didn't visit him in prison.

ADELE

He didn't want me to.

KAREN

Why not?

ADELE

I don't know. He was different after he was sentenced, looking at thirty years. Said it depressed him every time the younger cons called him an old-timer.

KAREN

But you spoke to him on the phone.

ADELE

He'd call every once in a while.

KAREN

He called the day he escaped.

ADELE

He did? I don't remember. Did he say about me? In the trunk?

KAREN

(*beat, lies*)

He said he wished the two of you could start over, live a normal life.

ADELE

Huh. Problem is, Jack's idea of a normal life is robbing banks. It's all he's ever done.

KAREN

Did you know that when you married him?

ADELE

He said he was a card player. I could live with that. I never knew he robbed banks till he got busted with that car that caught fire – if you can imagine something like that happening, comes out of the bank and the car's on fire. I did go see him in jail to tell him I was filing for divorce. He said, 'OK.' Jack's so easygoing.

(*pause*)

He was fun, but never what you'd call a real husband.

Adele looks out the window. Karen waits, looks to an end table where she sees a photograph of Jack and Adele on a boat somewhere ten years back.

I'll say one thing for Jack, he was never ugly or mean, or drank too much. He was very considerate, lights on or off, if you know what I mean.

KAREN

Really.

(*looking at the picture*)

Hm.

She realizes Adele is looking at her.

Adele, sooner or later, he's gonna get caught. I'd like to get him before he does something else, makes it worse on himself.

ADELE

Buddy'll take care of him. Keep him out've trouble. He's Jack's conscience. Always has been.

(*chuckles*)

He tell you how they met?

Karen shakes her head.

Jack came out of a bank he just robbed in Pasadena, couldn't get his stolen car to start. Battery was dead. He looks over, sees Buddy sitting in a burgundy Bonneville, goes up, offers him a thousand dollars for a jump. Turns out, Buddy was casing the same bank and saw the whole thing. Buddy says,

I'll take the thousand, but we're leaving in my car, not that piece of shit you come in.

(*pause*)

They musta robbed fifty banks together.

KAREN

Till they got busted.

ADELE

That wasn't Jack's fault. No, that was on account of Buddy, for some reason, decided to call his sister and confess to a job *before* they'd done it instead of after. She called the FBI and they both went down, ended up at Lompoc.

(*pause*)

I think Buddy felt kinda bad about that.

KAREN

Any idea where I could find Buddy? Or Glenn?

Adele looks at Karen, then jumps at the sound of three quick raps on the door.

CHINO'S VOICE

Adele? You in there?

ADELE

Yes.

CHINO

I want to speak with you, please.

ADELE

Who is it?

CHINO'S VOICE

I talk to the guy you work for, Emil. He tole me your number and where you live. See, I'm looking for an assistant and would like to speak to you.

ADELE

Oh. Uh-huh.

CHINO'S VOICE

You did work for Emil, right?

ADELE

Yeah, I was Emil's box-jumper for almost four years.

CHINO'S VOICE

You were his what, his box?

ADELE

His assistant.

Karen looks at the door. Something's wrong . . . Through the glass bricks that line one side of the door, we see blurred movement on the other side, someone doing something *. . .*

You say you perform in the Miami area?

CHINO'S VOICE

Yes, around here. I was a mayishan in Cuba before I come here. Manuel the Mayishan was my name.

And now Karen and Adele look at each other.

Can you open the door?

Karen shakes her head 'no'.

ADELE

I'm not dressed.

CHINO'S VOICE

Listen to me.

(*lowers his voice*)

I'm a good friend of Jack Foley.

Boom. Karen gets to her feet, brings her bag to the edge of the table, sees Adele staring at her.

KAREN

Ask him his name.

ADELE

Who are you?

CHINO'S VOICE

(*beat*)

José Chirino.

Karen brings her Beretta out of the bag.

Or maybe you hear Jack Foley call me Chino. I'm the same person.

Karen moves along the table to Adele.

KAREN

(*soft*)

Tell him to wait in the hall, you have to get dressed. Say it loud.

As Adele speaks, Karen racks the slide on her 9mm.

ADELE

Wait in the hall! I have to get dressed!

CHINO'S VOICE

Tell me where is Jack Foley, I don't bother you no more.

Karen motions for Adele to keep talking as she takes a position beside the door, where we now see Chino's silhouette in one of the three glass panels in the centre of the door.

ADELE

I don't know where he is.

CHINO'S VOICE

Listen, I'm the one help Jack escape from prison. He tole me, I can't find him to see you. So why don't you open this fucking door. OK? So we can speak.

ADELE

(*staring at Karen*)

Go away, or I'll call the police.

CHINO'S VOICE

Why you want to do that, to a frien'?

Adele says nothing. Then . . .

OK, you don't want to help me, I'm leaving.

(*pause*)

I'm going now. I see you maybe some time, OK? Bye-bye.

KAREN

(*low*)

Go in the bedroom and –

Suddenly, Chino's fist – wrapped in his shirt – explodes through one of the glass panels. Adele and Karen both jump as Chino pushes his arm through, reaches for the doorknob . . .

But Karen grabs the knob first and, using all of her weight as leverage, pivots and flings the door open with Chino's arm still sticking through the glass . . .

The force of this slingshots the man into the room, where he bangs against a wall and falls to the floor. Dazed, Chino reaches for his .22 as he now tries to get to his feet.

Karen brings up her Beretta in two hands, cocks it and puts the front sight on his chest.

Leave it where it is.

CHINO

(*frowning*)

Wait. You not Adele?

KAREN

I'm a federal marshal and you're under arrest. Put the gun on the table. I mean, now.

CHINO

Oh. Then this must be Adele . . .

He now aims the gun point-blank at Adele.

KAREN

Put it down or I'll shoot.

CHINO

You wouldn't shoot me, would you?

KAREN

What do you want to bet?

CHINO

(*beat*)

I could walk out of here.

KAREN

If you move, if you look at her again, you're dead.

Chino doesn't move. Keeps his gun on Adele. Karen starts walking towards him.

You can live or die, it's up to you.

CHINO

Oh, is that right? You going to shoot me? Nice girl like you?

(*smiles*)

I don't think so.

KAREN

You don't, huh?

And with that, she kicks him in the knee. Chino buckles over and she hits him on the side of the head with her gun.

On your knees.

He does as he's told. Karen raises his jacket, feels around his waist from behind.

Lie face down on the floor.

CHINO

(*hurting*)

What?!

She kicks him over on to his stomach and stays there. She puts her foot to his back as she reaches for the phone, dials. She sees Adele staring at her.

(*to Adele*)

Excuse me . . .

Karen looks at Adele a moment, then says into the phone . . .

KAREN

Daniel Burdon, please. Karen Sisco.

CHINO

Excuse me, Adele?

ADELE

Yes.

CHINO

You do the sawing of the box in half trick with you inside?

ADELE

(*beat*)

Yes.

CHINO

Tell me, how do you do that?

Adele looks at Karen, who shoves Chino's head to the floor with her foot.

KAREN

Shut up.

BURDON

(*phone*)

Karen. Where are you? I been trying to get a hold of you.

KAREN

Daniel. Listen –

BURDON

(*phone*)

Where are you? I been trying to reach you.

KAREN

I'm at Adele Delisi's.

BURDON

What – we already talked to her. That's a dead end.

KAREN

(*looking at Chino*)

Yeah, I know. I was just leaving. Why were you trying to reach me?

BURDON

There was a Buddy Bragg at Lompoc around the same time Foley was there. We got an address for him at the Adams Hotel in Hallandale. I want you to go there, see if you can get the manager to ID him as the other guy. If he does, you call me right away.

KAREN

All right, but . . .

BURDON

(*phone*)

But don't you *do* anything. You just have a seat, wait for me to get there.

KAREN

Sure, Daniel.

BURDON

(*phone*)

Now. What is it you wanted to tell me?

KAREN

Oh, I was just wondering, if I were to bring in Chirino, would you put me on the Task Force?

BURDON

(*phone, impatient*)

What? Is that what you're calling me about?

KAREN

Yes or no, Daniel. If I get him, will you let me go after Foley?

BURDON

(*phone*)

Yeah, sure, Karen. You bring in Chirino, you can be on the Task Force.

KAREN

That's all I wanted to know.

BURDON

(*phone*)

Good. Now forget about the ex-wife and get over to the Adams Hotel.

Karen hangs up, looks at Adele. Adele nods.

ADELE

You're good.

KAREN

Thank you.

INT. BUDDY'S APARTMENT. NIGHT

Foley and Buddy quickly pack up their stuff.

FOLEY

First thing we do, we get to Detroit, we find Glenn, then we find a window to throw him out of.

BUDDY

I been thinkin', if I was Glenn, I was up there to take down the Ripper, where would I go?

FOLEY

Well, first off, if you were Glenn, you wouldn't be thinking.

BUDDY

Remember Snoopy Miller, his old pal from Lompoc?

FOLEY

Snoopy. Christ, I thought he'd be brain-dead by now.

BUDDY

He isn't fighting no more. Glenn told me the Snoop's been managing some guys up there now, works out at the Kronk.

INT. SHALAMAR APARTMENTS. LOBBY. NIGHT

The ancient residents stop what they're doing as Burdon enters with eight guys in jackets and wool shirts hanging out, running shoes, half of them carrying what look like athletic bags. Karen meets them as they all walk to the elevator.

BURDON

You get the key?

KAREN

They're in 7D.

She hands it to him as they wait for the elevator.

BURDON

I want two men outside, front and back. Conway and Jessup go on up to seven, cover both ends of the hall.

Burdon, Karen and the remaining four SWAT team agents. Burden looks at them one at a time.

You're primary, you're secondary, you're point man.

KAREN

You're gonna use a ram?

BURDON

Yeah, why?

KAREN

The manager's door is metal.

They all look at her.

You know what I mean? They might all be. And a ram on a metal door makes an awful lot of noise for what good it does.

Burdon looks at her, not all that happy she spoke up. The fourth man raises the shotgun, a three-inch strip of metal taped to the muzzle.

FOURTH MAN

I got a shock-lock round in my shotgun oughta do the trick.

BURDON

Fine. Whatever.

He sees the elevator still hasn't come down.

Fuck it. Let's take the stairs. Karen . . .

Burdon pauses, looks at Karen, hands her a radio.

Take the radio, stay down here in the lobby, watch the elevator.

KAREN

What? Daniel, I wanna go upstairs.

BURDON

You can go wait out in the car, you want to.

She doesn't say anything.

Now you see Foley and this guy Bragg come in behind us, whatta you do?

KAREN

(*angry*)

Call and tell you.

BURDON

And you let them come up. You don't try to make the bust yourself. You understand?

Before she can answer, an old woman steps in, asks Burdon . . .

OLD WOMAN

Are you delivering the oxygen?

Burdon looks at her, then nods for his men to start up the stairs.

INT. THE SEVENTH FLOOR. DAY

Everyone's in position as Burdon eases the key into the lock, turns it. The door won't budge, a dead bolt holds it shut.

The guy with the shotgun puts the strip of metal against the seam, where the lock enters the frame, the muzzle of the shotgun exactly three inches now from the dead bolt, and looks over his shoulder at Burdon.

With the sound of the blast, we then . . .

CUT TO:

INT. ELEVATOR. DAY

Foley and Buddy ride down with an old lady. The doors open. The woman doesn't move.

BUDDY

Is this your floor, mother?

OLD LADY

Oh. Yes, it is.

INT. LOBBY. DAY

An old gent in a golf cap smiles at Karen sitting there on the couch in front of the elevator.

OLD GENT

Like to play some gin?

KAREN

No, thank you.

He creeps off towards the elevator.

INT. BUDDY'S APARTMENT. DAY

Burdon and his men fan out through the place.

INT. LOBBY. DAY

We hear Burdon's voice.

BURDON
(*radio*)
Karen. They're not up here. Keep your eyes open.

Karen looks off towards the street entrance, then back at the elevator where the man is still waiting, leaning on his cane.

The elevator door opens to reveal Buddy and Foley.

OLD GENT
Going up?

Buddy and Foley don't answer. The old man starts to get on, feeling with his cane, taking for ever.

Karen and Foley are staring at each other. He doesn't move. Not until the elevator door begins to close.

Buddy sees Karen, helps the old man aboard as . . .

Karen picks up her radio, is about to speak into it when . . .

Foley raises his hand. And waves as the door closes.

INT. ELEVATOR. DAY

The elevator resumes going down.

OLD GENT
Shit, I wanted to go up.

BUDDY
Let's just hope there's no one in the garage.

FOLEY

She looked right at me. She didn't yell or get excited. She didn't move.

INT. BUDDY'S CAR. DAY

They get in and Buddy starts the car.

BUDDY

They know where I live, I guess they know what I drive, so maybe we should pick up another car on the way.

FOLEY

She just sat there, looking right at me.

Buddy gives him a look, shakes his head and then burns rubber out of the garage as we . . .

CUT TO:

Close-up of Karen staring straight ahead.

BURDON

(*on the radio*)

Karen. Report. You see anything? Karen? You there? Karen . . .?

INT. AIRPORT TERMINAL. DAY

As Marshall walks Karen to the gate.

MARSHALL

He waved to you?

KAREN

I couldn't swear to it, but I'm pretty sure he did.

MARSHALL

You wave back?

KAREN

I didn't have time.

MARSHALL

I imagine you would've though.

She shakes her head.

KAREN

Buddy's sister Regina Mary Bragg got two calls from Buddy up in Detroit this morning, called Burdon. She's also the one gave Burdon Buddy's address.

MARSHALL

So?

KAREN

So what I want to know is why Buddy still calls his sister every week even after she turned him in.

MARSHALL

He doesn't seem to hold a grudge.

(*pause*)

What *I* want to know is why, they got such a big score up north, did Foley hang around Miami for so long?

(*looks at her*)

Any thoughts on that one?

KAREN

None I'd like to share.

She gives him a kiss

I'll call soon as I get in.

DISSOLVE TO:

EXT. BLOOMFIELD HILLS. DETROIT. DAY

Snow. Everywhere. A black Lincoln Town Car creeps through the neighbourhood full of big, beautiful snow-covered homes.

MAURICE

(*voice-over*)

I don't just manage fighters, or deal product any more . . .

INT. CAR. DAY

Glenn – sunglasses – sits in the back with Maurice, a.k.a. 'Snoopy' – wearing a purple bandanna and his own dark sunglasses.

MAURICE

I've diversified since the last time you saw me. I've vertically integrated and now I'm into home invasions and the occasional grand larceny.

Glenn just nods, stares out the window.

White Boy Bob's my all-around man, my bodyguard when I feel I need one, and my driver.

Maurice indicates White Boy Bob, a fucking huge, depraved-looking white guy now squeezed in behind the wheel.

Watch the road, boy.

(*pause*)

I like this Town Car. We can cruise the man's neighbourhood without getting the police or private security people on our ass.

GLENN

Sure, right, they see Bigfoot driving around a black guy wearing shades and a lavender fucking bandanna, no, they won't think anything of it.

MAURICE

It's lilac, man, the colour, and the style's made known by Deion and other defensive backs in the pros. I could be one of them living out here with doctors of my race and basketball players. OK, here comes Mr Ripley's house up on the left. Yeah. The brick wall. There's his drive, right there.

The car creeps past a huge Tudor-style country house.

You sure Foley and his pal aren't coming up here, do this themself?

GLENN

If they're not busted now, they're gonna be.

(*pause*)

It's wide open.

EXT./INT. CAR. MAURICE'S SHITTY NEIGHBOURHOOD IN DETROIT. LATER

People on the street with vacant expressions watch as the black Town Car moves past the broken-down homes, cars on blocks and snow-covered trash.

GLENN

So you still haven't said, how you wanna do it?

MAURICE

I'll show you, soon as I get one more guy I'm gonna need, Moselle's brother, Kenneth. Along with White Boy there.

GLENN

What?

The car pulls to the kerb and Kenneth – a wiry black man in a bright yellow T-shirt and red baseball cap backward, always seems to be high on some chemical or another – gets in.

MAURICE

You get everything?

Kenneth tosses a gym bag into the back seat. Glenn stares at it. Something about the bag makes him uneasy. Maybe it's the hacksaw that sticks partially out of the opening.

Cool. Kenneth, this is the man I told you about, Glenn.

KENNETH

The one gonna help us rip off the rich guy?

MAURICE

That's right.

GLENN

Help *you . . .*

White Boy Bob pulls out again. Glenn looks at the two psychos in front, then turns to Maurice.

Wait a minute. I'm letting *you* in on this, not all your friends.

MAURICE

You just ask me how we gonna do it. That's what I'm here for, tell you how. We the experts.

Glenn can't believe this is happening.

Thing I'm worried about is you.

GLENN

Me?

MAURICE

Yeah. If you can step up and actually do it. Understand? 'Stead of just talking the talk.

GLENN

Can I do what?

MAURICE

Walk in a house with me, do this cross-dressin' nigga named Eddie Solomon I used to sell to been dealin' on his own.

GLENN

What – when?

MAURICE

Right now, son.

GLENN

I don't have to prove shit to you. The Ripley job is *my* job. You're either in or you're not. You wanna pop some crack dealer pissed you off, that's your problem, not mine.

MAURICE

Look, Glenn, I know you cool, but you don't have to give me no tone of voice, OK? You don't like what I'm saying, you can get out anywhere along here you want.

GLENN

I think you're forgetting, this is my car. I drove it up here.

MAURICE

Hey, shit, come on. I say I want this car, man, it's mine. You go get yourself another one. I say I'm in on Ripley, I'm in, with or without *your* ass. I say I want you to come along on another job, see if you for real or not, guess what you gonna do?

Glenn looks at Maurice, now ice-cold behind the shades.

WHITE BOY BOB

We're here.

Glenn looks out the window as they pull up in front of a decrepit-looking two-storey house. Maurice opens the gym bag, passes the hacksaw and a hand axe up to White Boy Bob, a sawn-off shotgun to Kenneth, and takes out a big .45 for himself.

MAURICE

Let's go see Eddie.

Glenn hesitates, then slowly gets out of the car as we hear . . .

RIPLEY

(*voice-over*)

Must take balls, do what you do.

EXT. LOMPOC FPC. YARD. DAY

As Foley walks with Ripley across the yard.

RIPLEY

Tell me something. What's it like, walk in a bank with a gun, stick it up?

FOLEY

I don't know. I never used a gun.

RIPLEY

Really?

FOLEY

You'd be surprised what all you can get, you ask for it the right way.

RIPLEY

(*smiles*)

You're the reason, Jack, I don't keep all my money in banks.

FOLEY

No? Where do you keep it, Dick?

Ripley smiles.

I'm talking about all those uncut diamonds you told Glenn about.

RIPLEY

(*still smiling*)

I know what you're talking about.

FOLEY

You're the one with balls, Dick, say something like that to someone like Glenn. Or maybe you just forgot where you were for a minute.

RIPLEY

Yeah, but who's gonna believe Glenn? I mean, do *you* believe Glenn?

FOLEY

Of course not.

RIPLEY

Plus, even it was true, he'd still have to figure out where I keep 'em.

FOLEY

Doesn't have to figure out shit. You *told* him you keep 'em at your house.

RIPLEY

(*shrugs, big smile*)

It's a big house.

Ripley sits down on one of the picnic tables, looks around the yard.

Tell me something, Jack, how much longer you in here?

FOLEY

Twenty-two months, three days, two hours. Why?

RIPLEY

I was just thinking that I could use a guy like you, someone knows how to ask for things the right way. I'm talkin' about when you're outta here. I mean, you can't rob banks for ever.

Foley looks at Ripley.

FOLEY

It's a little late for me.

RIPLEY

Hey, Jack? Bullshit. I didn't make my first million until I was forty-two. Forty-two. You really *want* to change, it's never too late.

FOLEY

I don't know. I'm not exactly the nine-to-five type.

RIPLEY

Who is? But then you gotta look at a job as more than just work. You gotta look at it as peace of mind. As *security*, you know what I mean? I got offices in Detroit, Miami, Boston, take your pick.

FOLEY

My ex-wife's in Miami. It's nice down there.

RIPLEY

No need to decide now. Be like the fish. Let whatever happens happen.

FOLEY

The fish?

RIPLEY

Yeah, fish live in the present. They don't dwell on yesterday and they don't worry about tomorrow. Even when a big fish attacks a little fish, there's no neurosis involved. No guilt afterward. No whining on some fish-shrink's couch. They just do it. They accept.

FOLEY

I can't say that I've paid that much attention to 'em before.

RIPLEY

The fish saved my life. Two years ago, I found out I had high blood pressure. So my doctor, he tells me to go get an aquarium, look at the fish every time I felt myself stressing out.

FOLEY

And the guy sent you a bill for this?

RIPLEY

It works. You should try it some time.

FOLEY

The next time I walk into a bank.

Ripley shakes his head, then gets up . . .

RIPLEY

Think about my offer, Jack.

Foley watches him go.

BUDDY

(*voice-over*)

Hey, Jack . . .

CUT TO:

Close-up of Foley as he turns to us.

FOLEY

What?

We're inside a car across the street from the Kronk Recreation Centre – a red-brick building in a bleak, depressing neighbourhood.

BUDDY

You see this one . . .

Buddy reads from a newspaper while Foley watches the gym.

'Fight over tuna casserole may have spurred slaying.' Seems this woman's live-in boyfriend, seventy years old, complained about her tuna noodle casserole and she shot him in the face with a twelve-gauge. Police found noodles in the woman's hair and think the guy dumped the casserole dish on her before she shot him. They'd been together ten years.

FOLEY

Love is funny.

Buddy looks at him. Notices something over Foley's shoulder.

BUDDY

Hey –

And now Foley turns and looks over as the black Town Car pulls into the Kronk parking lot.

INT. TOWN CAR. DAY

Kenneth and White Boy Bob nod along to some rap tape in the front seat. Glenn sits in the back, looking pale, hugging himself, shaking. Maurice looks out the window . . .

MAURICE

Was a time you see a gold Mercedes over in the parking lot has a licence plate on it say 'HITMAN?', you know Tommy Hearns is inside. Seeing the car would get our juices flowing.

Maurice looks at Glenn now and grins.

You already got your juices flowing, huh? Pissed your pants back there at Eddie's house, didn't you?

Glenn just looks at Maurice.

That was some shit, huh?

GLENN

(*indicates Kenneth*)

Why'd he have to do that to that girl?

MAURICE

Yeah, Kenneth, why you have to do that to that poor girl.

KENNETH

(*smiles*)

Do what?

Glenn says nothing, just looks at Kenneth.

MAURICE

Just wait till we get inside Ripley's house.

And he and White Boy Bob start laughing as they get out of the car.

GLENN

It's all right with you, I'll just hang in the car.

MAURICE

(*beat*)

No. You gonna stay close to me from now on. So you don't disappear on me.

GLENN

Why would I do that?

Maurice looks at him, starts laughing. White Boy Bob and Kenneth join in. Maurice leans over . . . Glenn flinches as Maurice opens Glenn's jacket so that we can see the blood splattered on his T-shirt.

MAURICE

Was worse than you imagined, wasn't it?

(*pause, smiles*)

Baby, you with the bad boys now.

INT. FOLEY AND BUDDY'S CAR. DAY

As they watch Glenn and Snoopy and White Boy Bob get out of the car.

BUDDY

Whatta you think?

FOLEY

I think Glenn opened his big mouth and now we got us another partner.

BUDDY

Or two.

INT. BOXING GYM. DAY

Glenn sits on a bench near the rear wall, facing the ring. Kenneth grabs a magazine, walks into the john. A shirtless White Boy Bob lifts weights while Maurice moves around the ring calling to the boxers inside.

MAURICE

Stick and jab!

VOICE

Hey, Studs, how you doing?

He looks up, sees Buddy and Foley coming this way.

GLENN

Jesus Christ, what're you guys doing here?

They sit down on either side of him, close.

FOLEY

Weren't you expecting us?

GLENN

That broad you picked up – did you know she was a US Marshal, for Christ sake?

Now he turns to Buddy as Buddy stands up, takes off his overcoat and sits down again.

She *knew* me from some bullshit dope bust. She drove me to court. Twice. You know what she said, we're in the car on the turnpike? 'I never forget anybody I've cuffed and shackled.'

FOLEY

Yeah? She said that to you?

Glenn turns to see Foley with a mild expression on his face, almost smiling.

What happened to your shades? Someone finally step on 'em?

GLENN

(*touches his head*)

I don't know . . .

Foley notices the blood on Glenn's shirt.

FOLEY

Who's blood you got all over you?

GLENN

These guys, man, they're crazy.

(*looks off*)

Shit.

Foley follows his gaze, sees Maurice coming this way, White Boy Bob beside him, carrying his shirts.

FOLEY

Is that Snoopy? In the purple doo rag?

BUDDY

What's he do now, tell fortunes?

Maurice stands at the edge of the ring apron, looks from Foley to Buddy and back again, pretty serious about it.

WHITE BOY BOB

We have a problem here?

MAURICE

(*walking over*)

Jack Foley, famous bank robber.

FOLEY

Snoopy Miller, famous fight thrower.

MAURICE

It seems to me I been reading about you in the newspaper. Busted out of some joint in Florida, huh?

FOLEY

Low class of people there, Snoop.

WHITE BOY BOB

You call him that again I'll put your head through the wall.

BUDDY

What? You mean Snoop?

MAURICE

Nobody calls me Snoop no more or Snoopy, is what White

Boy's trying to say. He's a little crude, you understand. No, I left that Snoopy shit behind me.

BUDDY

But you call this bozo White Boy?

GLENN

White Boy Bob.

(*baiting*)

White Boy used to be a fighter.

BUDDY

What's he do now outside of shoot his mouth off?

White Boy Bob stares down Buddy, who couldn't give a shit.

FOLEY

Like being back in the yard, huh?

MAURICE

Just like it. Nobody backing down. You back down, you pussy. Tell me what you and Buddy doing up here in the cold?

FOLEY

Glenn didn't tell you?

GLENN

I thought you guys were busted.

FOLEY

Why? Just because you left us standing on the side of the road?

Foley looks at Glenn. Glenn shrugs, laughs nervously. Foley smiles, laughs with him, maybe a little too hard. Now Maurice starts laughing. Buddy, too. White Boy's lost, looking from one guy to the next as Foley gets up, faces Maurice, his smile going away as he says . . .

Look, Snoop, I don't know what Glenn promised you or what you think you're gonna get, but the deal is me and Buddy get half of whatever we take from Ripley, understand? How you and Glenn cut up the rest is up to you.

MAURICE

Let's go outside and talk.

FOLEY

What's the matter with right here? It's nice and warm.

MAURICE

Warm? Man, it's ninety-five degrees in here, sometimes a hundred – the way Emanuel always kep' it so his boys'd sweat, get lean and mean like Tommy Hearns. No, I ain't talking any business in here. To me this is holy ground, man. You understand? I got to be someplace anyway. Y'all want to talk, come to the fights tomorrow night, we'll sit down and look at it good. The State Theater.

Foley nods, then looks at Glenn as Buddy gets up.

FOLEY

We'll see you tomorrow then.

Maurice then watches as they walk out.

MAURICE

White Boy, how much is the reward on the man again?

WHITE BOY BOB

Ten gees.

MAURICE

Uh-huh.

(*pause*)

You recall, did it say dead or alive?

EXT. CRIME SCENE. NIGHT

The same decrepit two-storey place Maurice et al. hit earlier. Now it's a crime scene. A small crowd of neighbourhood gawkers stand just behind the yellow tape. A huge spotlight lights up the front yard.

Karen pulls up in her rental car, gets out and badges the visibly freezing cop at the tape, working crowd control.

KAREN

I'm looking for Ray Cruz.

COP

He's inside.

(*angry*)

With everybody else.

Karen ducks under the tape and starts up the walk. She pauses to watch as two coroner's assistants cover with a sheet a dead black woman who lies just below a broken upstairs window.

INT. HOUSE. NIGHT

Hell. Karen has to step over a body minus a face that lies in the doorway. Straight ahead on the stairs is another body, a man on his back, head down the stairs, shotgun blast to the chest. He wears a dress, now bunched up around his waist.

Congealed blood runs down the stairs. Cops and crime-scene techs are everywhere. Karen looks at the guy on the stairs.

VOICE

Called themselves the Youngboys.

Karen looks over as Raymond Cruz, a stocky, genial-looking detective, comes out of the kitchen.

CRUZ

Ironic, isn't it?

KAREN

How are you, Raymond?

CRUZ

Freezing. But I'm getting warmer.

He kisses her on the cheek. She indicates the body by the door.

KAREN

Quite a mess.

CRUZ

Yeah. And I thought everyone liked Eddie.

KAREN

Who?

CRUZ

Dude in the dress is Eddie Solomon, used to buy scag off a corner till he kicked it and found his happiness with crack and then started dealing himself. Word on the street was he was saving up for an operation.

KAREN

What is it with crack and transsexuals?

CRUZ

Yeah, Eddie was a real character. Had these girls cooked the rocks he called the Rockettes.

KAREN

Yeah. I saw one of 'em outside.

CRUZ

Yonelle. Looks like someone raped her, shot her, then threw her out the window.

(*shakes his head*)

Fuckin' animals.

This shuts them both up. Cruz indicates the door.

Let's get some air.

She starts to follow him out, pauses as she sees something on the ground . . .

A broken pair of sunglasses. Wraparound . . . a lot like the ones she remembers Glenn wearing. Karen stares at them a moment, then walks out.

EXT. CRIME SCENE. NIGHT

As Cruz and Karen walk to his car. Strobes flash as press photographers struggle to shoot the crime scene.

CRUZ

Other than we had so much fun the last time we worked together. You gonna tell me why you're comin' to me instead of the FBI?

KAREN

I report to the FBI, first thing they're gonna do is ask me to go get some coffee.

CRUZ

You know, I'm not in homicide any more.

KAREN

No, I didn't know that.

CRUZ

Yeah, I'm crimes against persons and property now, also sex crimes and child abuse.

KAREN

Detroit, you must be pretty busy.

CRUZ

Yeah, and, as you can see, home invasions are big, too.

KAREN

Listen, Raymond, a year ago, DEA had this guy Glenn Michaels on possession with intent but couldn't make it stick. In his statement, Glenn said he went up to Detroit to visit a friend and look into job opportunities – if you can believe that.

CRUZ

Who was the friend?

KAREN

Guy named Maurice Miller, also known as Snoopy, a former prizefighter.

CRUZ

Christ, I know Snoopy Miller. He's a fuckin' wackjob thinks he's Sugar Ray Leonard. Hangs out with a couple other Grade-A nutcases over on the Westside.

KAREN

I'll need a last known address.

CRUZ

That's fine, but I don't want you to talk to Miller alone.

KAREN

Come on, Raymond, I'm a federal officer, I'm armed.

He turns and looks at her.

CRUZ

Yes, you are. I'll call you tomorrow with the address.

As he gets into his car, we then . . .

CUT TO:

A newspaper. The crime scene from the night before. A shot of Karen and Ray Cruz as they exit the house. A headline reads 'Triple Murder' blah-blah-blah . . .

BUDDY

(*phone*)

You have the paper?

INT. FOLEY'S HOTEL ROOM. DAY

Foley, wearing a suit now, no shoes, no tie, looks at the newspaper photograph of Karen.

FOLEY

It's a terrific shot of her.

INT. BUDDY'S ROOM. DAY

Buddy looking at the same shot . . .

BUDDY

Outside of that.

Intercutting Foley and Buddy:

FOLEY

Doesn't say what she's doing up here, but I don't think it has anything to do with us.

BUDDY

She came up here on her vacation, 'cause she likes shitty weather.

Foley reaches in one of the bags from the Jewish Recycling Center and pulls out a tie.

FOLEY

I think she's after Glenn. The girl still with you?

BUDDY

They don't stay the night, Jack, 'less you pay for it.

FOLEY

You tell your sister about it?

BUDDY

Just hung up.

FOLEY

How long you talk to her?

BUDDY

Two hours.

FOLEY

How long were you with the girl?

BUDDY

Forty-five minutes.

FOLEY

You didn't tell your sister about Ripley, did you? 'Cause I don't wanna go through that again.

BUDDY

Forget about my sister. If Karen Sisco's tailing Glenn, we're fucked. Tomorrow night at the fights we all get picked up.

FOLEY

Let's drive by where we're meeting and have a look. Maybe take a look at Ripley's place while we're at it.

Foley hangs up. He faces the mirror, starts to tie his tie.

RIPLEY

(*voice-over*)

I guess next time I see you, you'll be wearing a suit and tie . . .

INT. RIPLEY'S CELL. DAY

Foley leans in the doorway watching as Ripley, dressed in a jogging suit, and under the watchful eye of a guard, gathers up his belongings. He's going home.

FOLEY

I still haven't made up my mind yet.

RIPLEY

What's to think about?

FOLEY

You goin' right back to work?

RIPLEY

First, I'm goin' to Israel for a year, study the Talmud, work on a kibbutz . . . then come back, maybe take some tennis lessons.

He tears a picture off the wall . . .

Here . . .

(*hands it to Foley*)

Something to remember me by.

Foley stares at the photograph of sea life.

It's not the real thing, but it's still nice to look at.

Foley looks at Ripley, who extends his hand.

See you on the outside, Jack.

INT. FOLEY'S HOTEL ROOM. DAY

Foley finishes tying his tie, stares into the mirror, takes in the overall effect.

FOLEY

(*smiles*)

Hi! I just broke outta jail!

His smile fades, he then sits down heavily on the bed, looks at the picture of Karen another moment, then sets the paper aside, grabs the Yellow Pages, flips to hotels and dials the phone . . .

VOICE

(*phone*)

Atheneum Hotel.

FOLEY

Karen Sisco, please.

VOICE

(*pause, then*)

I'm sorry, but there's no one by that name registered.

FOLEY

Thank you.

He dials the next number . . .

VOICE
(*phone*)

Best Western . . .

EXT. MAURICE 'SNOOPY' MILLER'S HOUSE. DAY

Red brick, showing its age. Karen rings the doorbell and then waits with her hands shoved into the pockets of her dark navy coat. The door opens to reveal Moselle in her green silk robe holding her arms close against the cold.

KAREN

Moselle Miller?

MOSELLE

What do you want?

KAREN

I'm looking for Maurice.

MOSELLE

You find him, tell him the dog got run over and I'm out of grocery money.

MALE VOICE

Moselle. Who you talking to?

MOSELLE

Lady looking for Maurice.

MALE VOICE

What's she want?

MOSELLE

Hasn't said.

KAREN

That's not Maurice?

MOSELLE

That's Kenneth, my brother. He's talking on the phone.

MALE VOICE

Ask what she want with him?

MOSELLE

You ask her. Maurice's business is none of *my* business.

Sounding tired or bored. She turns from the door and walks into the living room. Karen steps inside, pushes the door closed and steps into the foyer.

MALE VOICE

How do I know?

Karen peers into a study, a small room with empty bookcases, and sees Kenneth in his backward red baseball cap as he talks on the phone.

KENNETH

The State, huh. Who's fighting?

Karen walks into the living room, where Moselle sits on the sofa lighting a cigarette.

MOSELLE

You like to sit down?

KAREN

Thanks.

Karen takes a chair and looks around the room: dismal grey daylight in the windows, dark wood and white stucco, the fireplace full of trash, plastic cups, wrappers, a pizza box.

I'm looking for a friend of mine I think Maurice knows.

MOSELLE

You not with probation, one of those?

KAREN

No.

MOSELLE

You a lawyer?

KAREN

(*smiles*)

No, I'm not. Maybe you know him. Glenn Michaels?

Moselle draws on her cigarette, blows out a stream of smoke.

MOSELLE

Glenn? No, I don't know any Glenn.

KAREN

He said he stayed here last November.

MOSELLE

Here? In this house?

KAREN

He said he stayed with Maurice.

MOSELLE

Well, *he* ain't even here that much. I like to know where he goes, but at the same time I don't *want* to know, you understand?

KAREN

(*beat*)

Your dog was killed?

MOSELLE

Got run over by a car.

KAREN

What did you call it?

Moselle looks at the couch, where a mangled frisbee sits.

MOSELLE

Was a she, name Tuffy.

KAREN

(*nods, then*)

Where do you think I might find Maurice?

MOSELLE

I don't know – the gym, the fights. I *know* he don't miss the fights. Having some tomorrow night at the State Theater. He use to take me.

KAREN

The State Theater?

VOICE

What you want with Maurice?

Karen turns, see Kenneth standing in the arched entrance from the foyer.

MOSELLE

She looking for a man name of Glenn.

KENNETH

Did I ask you? Go on out of here. Do something with yourself.

He waits until Moselle gets up, not saying a word, walks away from them through the dining room. Karen watches him come towards her now in kind of an easy strut. She indicates the scar over his eyes.

KAREN

You're a fighter?

KENNETH

How you know that?

KAREN

I can tell.

KENNETH

I *was* . . .

He moves his head in what might be a feint.

Till I got my retina detached two time.

He's standing so close to her, Karen has to look up at him.

KAREN

What'd you fight, middleweight?

KENNETH

Light to super-middleweight, as my body developed. You go about what, bantam?

KAREN

Flyweight.

KENNETH

You know your divisions. You like the fights? Like the rough stuff? Yeah, I bet you do.

(*moves closer*)

Like to get down and tussle a little bit? Like me and Tuffy, before she got run over, we use to get down on the floor and tussle. I say to her, 'You a good dog, Tuffy, here's a treat for you.' And I give Tuffy what every dog love best. You know what that is? A bone.

(*real close*)

I can give you a bone, too, girl.

KAREN

You're not my type.

KENNETH

Don't matter. I let the monster out, you gonna do what it wants.

KAREN

Just a minute.

Her hand goes into her bag next to the chair.

KENNETH

Bring your own rubbers with you?

Her hand comes out of the bag holding what looks like the grip on a golf club. Kenneth grins at her . . .

What else you have in there, mace? Have a whistle, different kinds of female-protection shit?

Karen pushes out of the chair to stand with him face-to-face.

KAREN

I have to go, Kenneth.

She gives him a friendly poke with the black vinyl baton that's like a golf-club grip.

Maybe we'll see each other again, OK?

She steps aside and brushes past him. He grabs her left wrist.

KENNETH

We gonna tussle first.

Karen flicks the baton and sixteen inches of chrome steel shoots out of the grip. She pulls an arm's length away from him and chops the rigid shaft at his head, Kenneth hunching, ducking away . . .

God *damn* . . .

He lets go of her and Karen gets the room she needs, so that when he comes at her, she whips the shaft across the side of his head and he howls, stops dead, presses a hand over his ear.

What's wrong with you?

KAREN

You wanted to tussle, we tussled.

And she walks out. She sees Moselle standing there in the foyer. Karen looks at her a moment, puts the baton in her purse and comes out with a business card.

I wrote my hotel number on there – in case you run into Glenn.

Moselle slips the card into the pocket of her robe. Karen smiles at her and walks out the door.

EXT. RICHARD RIPLEY'S HOUSE. DAY

It's snowing pretty hard when Foley and Buddy pull up out front.

INT. BUDDY'S CAR. DAY

Buddy wipes the condensation off his window, so they can see the house.

BUDDY

Now that's a really big house.

FOLEY

Jesus, look at that wall. Place almost looks like a prison.

BUDDY

No doubt the man's got some big-ass security system.

FOLEY

Time comes, we knock on the door. See if he wants to talk about old times. Go in the easy way.

BUDDY

Yeah? You think he'll let us in, we got Snoopy and the muscle-bound asshole with us?

FOLEY

Who says anybody's gonna be with us? I say we go to the fights tomorrow, find out what the Snoop's big plan is, then go in ahead of those guys – *alone.*

BUDDY

Let Glenn deal with the Snoop, while we're off livin' the good life.

FOLEY

Tell me something, Buddy. You know anyone who's actually done one last big score and gone on to live the good life? 'Cause it occurred to me that everyone *talks* about doing it, but I don't know anyone who's actually gone and *done* it. Do you?

BUDDY
(*beat*)
What about that D. B. Cooper guy?

Foley looks at him.

I mean, they don't know for sure he's dead.
(*pause*)
Look, there's always a chance we'll walk out've there with nothing. I say let fate decide.

FOLEY
Let fate decide? What're you, the fuckin' Dalai Lama now?

BUDDY
My sister believes in fate, but not hell. That's why she stopped praying for the lost souls since you don't hear that much about purgatory any more. But every day she asks her boss to pray I don't fuck up. Whatta you think, you think there's a hell, Jack?

FOLEY
Yeah, it's called Glades Correctional Institution and I'm sure as shit not going back there or any place like it.

BUDDY
You might not have a choice.

Foley looks at him.

They put a gun on you, you'll go back.

FOLEY
They put a gun on you, you still have a choice, don't you?

Foley turns back to the house. And now we hear . . .

MR HEARN
(*voice-over*)
I think you're gonna fit right in . . .

INT. RIPLEY ENTERPRISES PERSONNEL OFFICE. DAY

The personnel guy, Mr Hearn, sits behind his desk, squeezing a grip exerciser and smiling warmly at Foley, who wears a shitty suit and tie.

MR HEARN

Now Mr Ripley and I have had a long discussion about your role in the company and it was his feeling that you would be happiest working down here in Miami. How's that sound to you?

FOLEY

Great.

Mr Hearn pauses, looks down at Foley . . .

MR HEARN

You're about a 42 long, right?

FOLEY

What?

But Mr Hearn walks out without answering. Foley looks at the desktop, where a spoon sticks out of a half-eaten fruit-on-the-bottom yogurt, which in turn sits beside a half-eaten PowerBar.

Foley shakes his head, takes out his Zippo, starts to play with it.

MR HEARN

OK. Let's see how she fits.

Foley turns as Mr Hearn bounces back into the room with what looks like a uniform draped over one arm.

FOLEY

What is this?

MR HEARN

Your uniform.

FOLEY

My what?

Mr Hearn shows him the yellow patch that reads SECURITY *on one arm. Foley smiles . . . amused . . . angry . . . hurt . . .*

Are you kidding me?

INT. RICHARD RIPLEY'S OFFICE. DAY

View. Wet bar. Huge fucking aquarium.

RECEPTIONIST

(*off-screen*)

Sir, you can't go in there . . .

Ripley looks up from his desk as Foley steps in, the receptionist right behind him now.

RIPLEY

Jack? Whoa – what's the problem? Take it easy, let's talk . . .

Meanwhile, Ripley pushes a panic button beneath his desk.

FOLEY

A security guard? Are you fucking kidding me?

Ripley considers Foley a moment, then . . .

RIPLEY

You know, I wasn't sure you'd show up. But I was pretty sure that, if you did, you'd throw the job in my face.

(*pause*)

Understand something, Jack. Up to this point, everything you've done with your life means absolutely nothing in the real world. Less than nothing.

Foley says nothing.

You're a bank robber. This is not a marketable skill. There are no old bank robbers out in the world living on pensions. You know this. That's why you're here right now.

Still Foley says nothing.

Today, I'm offering you a lousy job at a lousy wage. You think you're better than that? Fine. Show me. Show me that you're really willing to change and we'll talk about something better. A lot better. But first, Jack, you gotta earn it.

FOLEY

How, Dick? The way *you* earned it? By marrying some rich broad owns the company, selling it off a piece at a time, then divorcing her? What is this Knute Rockne, pull yourself up by the bootstraps bullshit? Back in prison, guy like you, place like that, you were ice cream for freaks. You were a goddamn dumpling. Maurice and a dozen other guys coulda bled you till you had nothing. Till you *were* nothing. I saved your ass. So you'll pardon me if I don't wanna sit on a fuckin' stool all day saying 'Sign in here, please' or 'Hey, pal, you can't park there.' OK, Dick? I can't do it.

RIPLEY

Jack, I'm disappointed. I guess I misjudged you.

Two massive security guards appear in the doorway.

FOLEY

Hey, what job he promise *you* guys?

GUARD

There's two ways we can do this.

FOLEY

Yeah? What are they?

RIPLEY

Gentlemen. I think we've calmed down now. Haven't we, Jack?

FOLEY

Oh, yeah, I'm calm. In fact, I'm totally 'relaxed . . .'

And with that he picks up a paperweight (a lead fish) and wings it at the aquarium, shattering the glass.

EXT. RIPLEY'S BUILDING. FLORIDA. DAY

Foley is physically thrown out of the building by the two guards. He picks himself up. He kicks at the guards, who wave him off, go back inside.

Foley then starts down the steps, pauses as he sees . . .

The bank across the street we saw at the opening. Foley looks at it a moment, then calmly starts to take off his tie, drops it in the gutter as he starts across the street . . .

CUT TO:

INT. BUDDY'S CAR. DAY

As Buddy pulls away from the house, Foley pulls out the clipping of Karen he tore out of the morning paper. He's written the name 'Westin' on it.

FOLEY

Listen, I gotta get some better shoes, few other things before tomorrow. Why don't you drop me off at the Ren Cen, we'll hook up later?

BUDDY

Yeah, and I better call my sister.

CUT TO:

THE SNOWSTORM

It's really coming down. We then pull back to reveal we're looking out of a window inside the cocktail lounge at the top of the Westin.

A table of three young executive-looking guys in suits are laughing at something until Karen is ushered by a waitress to an adjacent table.

KAREN

Jack Daniel's, please, water on the side.

She turns, sees her reflection in the glass against the overcast sky, snow swirling, blowing in gusts, seven hundred feet above the city, down there somewhere.

EXECUTIVE GUY'S VOICE

Celeste, do us again, please, and put the lady's drink on our bill.

She turns to see them raising snifter glasses to her, smiling, pleasant-looking guys in dark suits.

KAREN

Thanks anyway.

WAITRESS

(*drifting over*)

They want to buy you a drink.

KAREN

I get that. Tell them I'd rather pay for my own.

She then watches the three guys looking at the waitress delivering the message. Then they look at Karen. She gives them a shrug, turns to watch the snow. Her drink arrives. She takes a sip, looks up as one of the guys comes over.

EXECUTIVE GUY

Excuse me. My associates and I made a bet on what you do for a living.

She glances at the table, the other two watching.

And I won. Hi, I'm Philip.

KAREN

If it's OK with you, Philip, I'd like to just have a quiet drink and leave. OK?

PHILIP

Don't you want to know what I guessed? How I know what you do for a living?

KAREN

Tell you the truth, I'm not even mildly curious. Really, I don't want to be rude, Philip, I'd just like to be left alone.

She turns back to the snowstorm. She sees his reflection turn and leave. A moment later, the next one appears at the table.

SECOND EXECUTIVE GUY

I think I know why you're depressed – if I may offer an observation.

She just looks at him. So sure of himself.

I have a hunch you're the new sales rep and your customer isn't exactly knocked out by the idea of a young lady, even one as stunning as you, handling the account. Am I close? Hi, I'm Andy.

She says nothing to him.

ANDY

We're ad guys. We flew in from New York this morning to pitch Hiram Walker Distillery, present this test-market campaign for their new margarita mix. What we do, we show this guy who looks like a Mexican bandido, you know, with the big Chihuahua hat, the bullet belts –

KAREN

Andy? Really. Who gives a shit?

He gives her a sympathetic expression.

ANDY

Want to tell me what happened?

KAREN

Beat it, will you?

She stares at the guy until he turns away. She sips her drink, stares once more out at the blizzard. After a few moments, another dark suit appears, reflected in the window.

VOICE

Can I buy you a drink?

Boom. Not one of the executive guys. She stares at the reflection for a moment, then slowly turns, looks up at Jack Foley now standing there in his new navy-blue suit.

KAREN

(*beat*)

Yeah, I'd love one.

(*pause*)

Would you like to sit down?

He pulls the chair out, looking at her. The three guys at the other table now staring as he sits down. Foley offers his hand.

FOLEY

I'm Gary.

She hesitates, then shakes his hand.

KAREN

I'm Celeste.

She smiles with him. When she lowers her hand to the table, his hand comes down to cover hers. She watches his expression as she brings her hand out slowly, his eyes not leaving hers, and lays her hand on his. The tips of her fingers brush his knuckles lightly, back and forth.

It takes hours to get a drink around here. There's only one waitress.

FOLEY

I can go to the bar.

KAREN

Don't leave me.

FOLEY

Those guys bother you?

KAREN

No, they're all right. I meant, you just got here.

She picks up her drink and places it in front of him.

Help yourself.

She watches him take a sip, smack his lips.

FOLEY

You like bourbon?

KAREN

Love it.

FOLEY

(*passes the glass back*)

Well, we got that out of the way.

(*pause*)

Tell me, Celeste. What do you do for a living?

KAREN

I'm a sales rep. I came here to call on a customer and they gave me a hard time because I'm a girl.

FOLEY

Is that how you think of yourself?

KAREN

What, as a sales rep?

FOLEY

A girl.

KAREN

I don't have a problem with it.

FOLEY

I like your hair. And that suit.

KAREN

I had one just like it – well, it was the same idea, but I had to get rid of it.

FOLEY

You did?

KAREN

It smelled.

FOLEY

Having it cleaned didn't help, huh?

KAREN

No.

(*pause*)

What do you do for a living, Gary?

FOLEY

(*beat*)

How far do we go with this?

This stops her, throws her off balance.

KAREN

Not yet. Don't say anything yet. OK?

FOLEY

I don't think it works if we're somebody else. You know what I mean? Gary and Celeste, Jesus, what do they know about anything?

KAREN

It's your game. I've never played this before.

FOLEY

It's not a game. Something you play.

KAREN

Well, does it make sense to you?

FOLEY

It doesn't have to, it's something that happens. It's like seeing a person you never saw before – you could be passing on the street – you look at each other and for a few seconds, there's a kind of recognition. Like you both know something. But then the next moment the person's gone, and it's too late to do anything about it, but you remember it because it was right there and you let it go, and you think, 'What if I had stopped and said something?' It might happen only a few times in your life.

KAREN

Or once.

They look at each other a moment, then . . .

FOLEY

Why don't we get out of here.

They both get up. The ad guys at the table watch as she follows Foley to the elevator. Karen winks at them.

INT. ELEVATOR. NIGHT

As they ride down to Karen's room. She looks at him, looks away. The doors open and they exit.

INT. KAREN'S HOTEL SUITE. NIGHT

He follows her in. She walks to the bar, fixes them each a drink. He checks out the room, takes in her view.

KAREN

How'd you find me?

He comes over to her, takes out the newspaper clipping with her picture and shows it to her.

Oh, God . . .

FOLEY

I called your room from downstairs.

KAREN

If I had answered, what were you gonna say?

FOLEY

Well, I'd say who I was and do you remember me and ask if you'd like to meet for a drink.

KAREN

If I remembered you. I came looking for you. I would've said sure, let's do it. But for all you knew I could show up with a SWAT team. Why would you trust me?

FOLEY

It would be worth the risk.

She looks at him, touches his face with her hand . . .

KAREN

You like taking risks.

FOLEY

So do you.

He kisses her now, puts his arms around her.

KAREN

What's the hurry, Jack? You have to be somewhere?

She hands him his drink. They both drink, then . . .

Sooner or later . . .

She stops and he looks at her over the rim of her glass.

You really wear that suit.

FOLEY

That's not what you were about to say.

She shrugs, lets it go. He puts down his drink, kisses her. She lets him, then moves to the couch.

KAREN

Remember how talkative you were? In the trunk? Adele said you do that when you're nervous.

FOLEY

She did, huh.

KAREN

You kept touching me, feeling my thigh.

FOLEY

Yeah, but in a nice way.

He sits down and they kiss again. This time she peels his jacket off. He does the same with hers. He's starting to unbutton her blouse when –

I might've smelled like a sewer, but you could tell I was a gentleman. They say John Dillinger was a pretty nice guy.

KAREN

He killed a police officer.

He stops. Looks at her.

FOLEY

I hear he didn't mean to. The cop fell as Dillinger was aiming at his leg and got him through the heart.

KAREN

You believe that?

FOLEY

Why not?

She looks at him, decides to get off this subject. Anyway he's finished unbuttoning her blouse and is now putting his hands inside her shirt. She closes her eyes.

KAREN

You know that Sig .38 you took was my favourite. My father gave it to me.

As he kisses her on the neck.

What were you gonna do with me?

FOLEY

I don't know. I hadn't worked that part out yet. All I knew was that I liked you, and I didn't want to leave you there, never see you again.

KAREN

You waved to me in the elevator.

She's loosening his tie, unbuttoning his shirt.

FOLEY

I wasn't sure you caught that.

KAREN

I couldn't believe it. I was thinking of you by then, a lot, wondering what it would be like if we did meet. Like if we could take a time-out . . .

FOLEY

Really? I was thinking the same thing. If we could call time and get together for a while.

They look at each other a moment.

You know I saw you on the street.

KAREN

Where?

FOLEY

Outside Adele's.

He starts to kiss her again, but –

KAREN

You were going to see her?

FOLEY

To warn her about Chino.

KAREN

So she did help you?

FOLEY

I don't think we should get into that.

KAREN

No, you're right. Or Buddy. I won't ask if he's with you or what you're doing here in Detroit. Or if you've run into Glenn Michaels yet.

FOLEY

Don't talk like that, OK? You scare me.

And he moves to kiss her, but she stands up, holds out her hand.

KAREN

Come on.

He gets up and she leads him across the room.

INT. BEDROOM. NIGHT

Jack sits on the bed to take off his shoes, stands up to take off his pants.

KAREN

Are you gonna leave your tie on?

He looks at her, down to her bra and panties, watches as she gets out of the rest of her clothes and comes over to him, standing close to help him with the tie.

FOLEY

My God, look at you.

When her clothes are off, she loops the tie around his neck again and then as she turns off the light . . .

She kisses him. He sits down on the bed, drawing her back with him, the only light now coming from the sitting room.

You having fun?

She smiles and then they start to make love as we then . . .

FADE OUT

CUT TO:

Karen eyes open, serious now.

She's lying in Jack's arms. She looks at him a moment, then moves away from him to sit up and swing her legs off the bed.

FOLEY

You coming back?

KAREN

I'm just going to the bathroom.

She gets up and crosses the room to the bathroom and closes the door. Foley picks up his Zippo off the night table.

INT. BATHROOM. NIGHT

She comes in. Looks at herself in the mirror. Suddenly feels self-conscious. She grabs a bathrobe off the door.

INT. BEDROOM. NIGHT

Foley lies there, fiddling with the Zippo, staring up at the ceiling. She comes out again and stands looking down at him.

KAREN

I want you to know something. I wasn't looking for just a fuck, if that's what you're thinking.

FOLEY

Why are you mad?

KAREN

Or I did it for some kind of kinky thrill. Score with a bank robber the way some women go for rough trade.

FOLEY

What about *my* motive? Now I can say I fucked a US Marshal. You think I will?

KAREN

I don't know.

He raises the covers, but she just stands there.

FOLEY

I know of a guy he goes in the bank holding a bottle he says is nitroglycerin. He scores some cash off a teller, he's on his way out when he drops the bottle. It shatters on the tile floor, he slips in the stuff, cracks his head and they've got him. The nitro was canola oil. I know more fucked-up bank robbers than ones that know what they're doing. I doubt one in ten can tell a dye pack when he sees one. Most bank robbers are fucking morons. To go to bed with a bank robber for kinky thrills, as you say, you'd have to be as dumb as they are. I know you're not dumb, so why would I think that? Why would *you* think I might think that?

She comes over and sits down on the bed.

KAREN

You're not dumb.

FOLEY

I don't know about that. You can't do three falls and think you have much of a brain.

They lie there for a few moments, Karen watching him. He senses this, looks at her.

You getting serious on me now?

KAREN

I'm trying not to. I just wanna know what's gonna happen.

FOLEY

(*beat*)

You know.

And he kisses her.

EXT. DETROIT. DAY

The sun is out. The snow has stopped falling. A white blanket covers everything.

INT. KAREN'S HOTEL ROOM. DAY

Karen opens her eyes, wakes up. She closes them again, lies on her side, but doesn't move for a moment. Then . . .

KAREN

Oh, for Christ sake, grow up.

She opens her eyes and rolls on to her back. She turns her head: Foley's gone. She gets out of bed.

INT. SITTING ROOM. DAY

Karen comes into the room tying her robe. She looks at the coffee table where . . .

Something wrapped in a napkin lies by the half-empty bottle and the ice bucket. She picks it up and slowly unfolds the 'gift' from Foley: her Sig-Sauer .38.

INT. FOLEY'S HOTEL ROOM. DAY

Buddy stands at the window looking out as Foley – in his underwear – sits at the table reading the newspaper, a room-service breakfast, a bottle of Jim Beam close by.

BUDDY

It took you, what, seven hours to buy a pair of shoes?

FOLEY

I saw Karen Sisco.

Buddy turns to him.

BUDDY

And she saw you?

FOLEY

Yes, she did.

BUDDY

So how's that work, a wanted felon socializing with a US Marshal?

FOLEY

You know how I felt about her.

BUDDY

Did you give her a jump? If you did I might begin to understand where your head's at.

FOLEY

It wasn't about getting laid. I just wanted to know what might've happened if things were different.

BUDDY

You find out?

FOLEY

Yeah, I did.

Buddy watches Foley pour a shot of Jim Beam in his coffee.

BUDDY

So what's that mean? That you're disappointed by what you found or you're sorry you robbed all those banks?

FOLEY

I don't know.

INT. KAREN'S HOTEL ROOM. DAY

Karen sits there staring at a Wild Turkey bottle, a couple of glasses. She reaches for the phone, dials. A moment later, we hear Marshall Sisco's answering machine and she hangs up.

INT. STATE THEATER. NIGHT

A ring set up onstage. Men hang out on the side. Where movie seats used to be are rows of round nightclub tables; a row of them on each of four levels rising a step at a time up through the theatre to the bar. Rap music booms out of speakers as fighters are announced.

Everyone in here is black except for Glenn and White Boy Bob, who sit at a table in the front row, while Maurice, in shades and a dude black felt cap set on his head just right, walks along the apron of the stage.

MAURICE

Stick and jab, stick and jab!

White Boy Bob throws down a beer and gives Glenn's shoulder a jab.

WHITE BOY BOB

You drink like a girl.

White Boy Bob looks around to see if there are any other morons sitting nearby who think it's funny. Kenneth comes through for his pal and laughs.

INT. STATE THEATER. NIGHT

Karen walks through the bar, pauses as she sees Glenn sitting with White Boy and Kenneth. She steps back into the shadows as Glenn glances anxiously about.

Glenn pushes his chair back.

GLENN

I got to go take a piss.

He hesitates, sees the car keys on the table in front of White Boy Bob. But before he can grab them . . .

WHITE BOY BOB

What're you telling us for? You want somebody to hold your little pecker?

Glenn gets up, sees his coat on the back of the chair, but knows he can't take it with him. He walks away from the table.

EXT. STATE THEATER – PARKING LOT. NIGHT

Glenn exits the theatre and crosses to the parking lot. Karen exits right after, watches him get into the Town Car.

INT. TOWN CAR. NIGHT

Glenn, behind the wheel, half-lying on his right side as he tries to rip open the locked glove compartment. His head jerks around as Karen opens the door. He sits up straight as she gets in with him.

KAREN

Glenn, are you trying to steal this car?

GLENN

Jesus, I don't believe it.

KAREN

Another one of those days, huh, nothing seems to go right?

He raises his empty hands.

GLENN

I don't have the keys.

KAREN

I see that.

GLENN

I mean I'm not stealing the fucking car.

KAREN

You're not?

GLENN

I already stole it. Last week or whenever it was, in West Palm. I can't be stealing it again, can I?

KAREN

The two guys you were with – that one, that isn't Maurice Miller, is it? I've seen Snoopy's mug shot and that didn't look like him.

GLENN

Jesus. How'd you know about Snoopy?

Karen looks at him, shakes her head.

KAREN

Glenn, I know your life history, who your friends are, where you've been and now, it looks like, where you're going. Put your hands on the wheel.

GLENN

You're gonna bust me for picking up a car?

KAREN

For the car, for aiding and abetting a prison escape, and conspiring to do whatever you came here for.

GLENN

Listen, these guys, they're gonna be out here any minute looking for me. They're fucking animals.

KAREN

What's going on, Glenn?

GLENN

Nothing. I just wanna get the fuck outta here.

KAREN

But I thought the whole thing was your idea?

GLENN

Rippin' off Ripley was my idea, but these guys, man, they're into shit I can't handle.

KAREN

Ripley? You mean the Wall Street guy?

GLENN

Yeah, the plan was to pick him up at his office tomorrow, take him out to his house in Bloomfield Hills. Now, I don't give a shit what they do.

KAREN

And is Foley a part of this?

GLENN

He's supposed to be, but he hasn't shown up yet, which is a good thing for him.

KAREN

Why's that?

GLENN

Maurice is gonna kill him, try and collect the reward.

KAREN

(*beat*)

But you say he hasn't shown up, you think he backed out?

GLENN

I don't know – he doesn't exactly confide in me.

KAREN

Gee, I wonder why not.

GLENN

I'm freezing my ass off.

KAREN

You want to get out of here, run, it'll warm you up.

GLENN

Really?

KAREN

But listen, Glenn. If you're lying to me . . .

GLENN

I know, you'll find me. Jesus, I believe it. I keep thinking if you hadn't driven me to federal court last summer, you wouldn't even know who I am.

KAREN

If I didn't know you, Glenn, by tomorrow you'd be in jail or dead. Look at it that way. Go on.

And he takes off. She sits there another moment, then flicks her cigarette out the door, gets out the car.

EXT. PARKING LOT. NIGHT

Karen looks across the street at the theatre, sees people leaving. A few seconds later, she steps behind a car and watches as Buddy and Foley pull into the lot.

INT. STATE THEATER. NIGHT

Maurice sits with White Boy and Kenneth as Foley and Buddy come down the aisle to their table.

MAURICE

Where you been? You miss the big boys, come in time for the walkout fights. Well, shit, you may as well pull up a chair.

Foley and Buddy remain standing.

Kenneth, this is Mr Jack Foley and this is Mr Buddy, famous bank robbers.

Foley nods to the raincoat draped over the back of a chair.

FOLEY

Who's sitting here?

MAURICE

Your homie, Glenn. Only thing, he went to the men's about a while ago and never came back.

Foley gives Buddy a look. White Boy Bob grins at them.

WHITE BOY BOB

I think he must've fell in.

MAURICE

I sent these two looking for him, they come back shaking their heads.

FOLEY

Well, if he left his coat and he's been gone a while.

WHITE BOY BOB

The car's still there. I looked.

MAURICE

(*to the ring*)

Reggie, push off and hit, man. Push him off.

FOLEY

We're leaving.

MAURICE

The fuck you talking about?

FOLEY

Snoop, if you don't know where Glenn is . . .

Maurice takes Foley by the arm, moves him away from the table.

MAURICE

Look, what you worried about Glenn for? What's he know?

FOLEY

I thought everything.

Foley watches the fighters: one of them patient, moving in while the other one takes wild swings and misses . . .

MAURICE

Glenn knows everything we suppose to do *tomorrow*. Glenn could tell somebody that, yeah, but it don't mean shit. You understand? 'Cause Glenn don't know I changed the plan.

(*pause*)

It's happening tonight.

Foley looks at Maurice now.

Soon as we leave here. Stop home and pick up what we need and go do it.

FOLEY

(*beat*)

Give me a minute, talk to Buddy.

MAURICE

You got two minutes, that's all. Make up your mind.

FOLEY

I wasn't asking permission.

Foley walks up to the bar with Buddy.

They want to go tonight, before Glenn gets in any trouble, opens his big mouth.

BUDDY

Whatta you wanna do?

Foley takes out his lighter, begins playing with it.

You know they gonna set us up.

FOLEY

I get that feeling, yeah.

BUDDY

But you still think you can get the diamonds 'fore they do?

Foley looks at him a moment, then . . .

FOLEY

I'll make you a deal. Get out of here. Right now. I'll do the job with the Snoop, meet you wherever you want and give you half.

BUDDY

Half for doing what?

FOLEY

Getting me out of Glades for starters.

BUDDY

And who watches your back?

CUT TO:

Maurice as he sits down with White Boy Bob and Kenneth, watching Buddy and Foley talk up at the bar.

MAURICE

Man has all that reward on his head and still talks like a con in the yard. You know what I'm saying? Like he's a man you don't mess with. Yeah, well, what I say to Jack Foley is buuulls*hit.*

EXT. MAURICE'S HOUSE. NIGHT

It's snowing as Maurice, White Boy Bob, Kenneth, Buddy and Foley pile into the back of a van, the name of some plumbing and heating company on the side.

We pull back to reveal that we're watching from inside Karen's car. She waits for the van to pull away, then follows.

INT. VAN. NIGHT

Kenneth – the fucking maniac – at the wheel. Buddy and Foley piled into the back of the van full of plastic pipe and equipment. Maurice pulls on a pair of white coveralls.

FOLEY

That what they're wearing these days to break and enter?

MAURICE

Break and enter, shit. Take it and git, how it's done. Don't waste any time. That's how you do it.

FOLEY

So you've done this before, huh?

MAURICE

Shit, yeah. White Boy even got busted for it.

(*pause*)

White Boy, tell these boys the reason you went down on that burglary that time.

WHITE BOY BOB

I left my wallet in the house I robbed.

The guy grins at them. Foley can't believe it.

MAURICE

Takes the TV, the VCR, some other shit and leaves his wallet on the floor.

FOLEY

That's a wonderful story, Snoop. I'm very excited about tonight.

MAURICE

Hey. You learn from doing.

Foley and Buddy exchange looks. Maurice turns around, a Beretta in his hand. Foley looks at him. Buddy tenses.

You know how to use one a these?

FOLEY

I've seen 'em used on TV.

Maurice hands Foley the Beretta. Then reaches into a bag, comes up with a .38 he hands to Buddy.

INT. KAREN'S CAR. NIGHT

Karen tries to keep up with the van. But with the snow and the way Kenneth drives, she starts to lose them. She speeds up around a corner and loses control of the car.

EXT. STREET. NIGHT

Karen's car does a 360 in the ice and snow.

INT. VAN. NIGHT

Buddy and Foley are jostled about the back from Kenneth's insane driving.

BUDDY

Slow down.

Kenneth grins in the mirror, punches it more. Buddy gets out the .38 and touches it to the back of Kenneth's head.

Get ready to grab the wheel when I shoot this asshole.

Kenneth, his eyes freaked with speed, glares at Buddy in the mirror.

MAURICE

Do like he says, man. Slow down.

EXT. KAREN'S CAR. NIGHT

A pissed-off Karen gets out of her car, watches the van disappear.

KAREN

Shit –

INT. KAREN'S CAR. NIGHT

She takes out her cellphone, punches a number, reorients her car at the same time.

EXT. RICHARD RIPLEY'S HOUSE. NIGHT

The van creeps by one way, then the other, then pulls into the driveway.

INT./EXT. VAN/RIPLEY'S HOUSE. NIGHT

All five of them in the back end of the van now, bumping into each other until Maurice lets White Boy Bob out the rear end, leaving the doors open enough so he can watch. He then racks the slide on a .45.

MAURICE

'An army .45 will stop all jive.' Huey P. said that.

BUDDY

You think he was talking about walking into people's houses when he said it?

Maurice looks at Buddy. Buddy holds his gaze. Then the coach lights on either side of the front entrance come on.

MAURICE

(*pulls his mask down*)

Get ready to go skiing.

Now the front door opens . . .

Here we go.

We catch a glimpse of a woman in the doorway, arms folded over her bathrobe as White Boy Bob gives her a push and steps inside the house with her.

Maurice is out of the truck and Kenneth, with a shotgun, is scrambling to be next. Buddy catches him by his jacket collar and holds him squirming until Foley is out.

The minute Kenneth's feet hit the driveway he turns the twelve-gauge on Buddy, still in the truck. Foley takes the barrel in one hand and shoves it straight up in Kenneth's face.

FOLEY

Go on in the house before you get hurt.

Kenneth puts his face up close to Foley's and stares at him good before going inside. Foley turns to Buddy.

There's still time, take me up on my offer.

BUDDY

I'm not leaving you alone with these assholes.

INT. HOUSE. FOYER. NIGHT

Maurice has the woman back against a table. She's in her forties, with thick red hair hanging free. She looks ready to take a swing at whoever approaches.

WOMAN

I work here. I'm the maid.

Kenneth reaches out, opens her robe and we get a flash of flimsy bra and low-cut panties before she slaps him away.

WOMAN/MAID

Fuck off.

KENNETH

Hey, shit, we're gonna have a party.

MAURICE

Not yet. Where's Mr Ripley?

MAID

I told you, he isn't here.

MAURICE

Out for the evening?

MAID

He's in Florida. Palm Beach.

MAURICE

(*beat*)

When's he due back?

FOLEY

Jesus Christ, what difference does it make?You want to wait for him?

MAID

Mr Ripley's down for the season. Christmas to Easter.

MAURICE

You here all by yourself?

MAID

(*beat*)

That's right, just me.

Foley catches the hesitation, glances at Buddy.

MAURICE

Where's Ripley's safe at, he keep his valuables in.

MAID

I don't have any idea.

MAURICE

Let's go upstairs, have a look at the man's bedroom. All right now, you and Mr Buddy check the rooms down here. Look at the wall behind any pictures hanging on it. Look at the walls in the closets. The man has a safe, it's gonna be up there somewhere.

FOLEY

How about his place in Florida? If you'd called, we could've checked his walls down there before we left. That is, if you'd checked to see where he was. You follow me?

Maurice gives him a look, then pulls the maid up the stairs. Kenneth and White Boy Bob follow.

MAURICE

You set off any kind of alarm and you're a dead Hazel. Understand?

Kenneth puts his arm around the maid.

KENNETH

What's you name, mama?

He hooks a finger in the waist of her panties, pulls on the elastic, is about to look in there when Maurice backhands him across the face.

MAURICE

First money, then pussy.

Alone with Buddy now, Foley rolls his mask up on his head.

FOLEY

You ever wear one of these?

BUDDY

I don't ski.

FOLEY

Stay with the maid. I'm gonna have a look around.

INT. KAREN'S CAR. NIGHT

Karen on the phone – snow falling all around her.

RAYMOND CRUZ

(*phone*)

I'll send a unit over there, see if there's anything going on.

KAREN

Tell me where Ripley's house is. I'll meet them there.

CRUZ

(*phone*)

Karen, you gonna promise me you're not gonna go in, do anything stupid till I get there.

INT. BEDROOM. NIGHT

Full of fat, cushy chairs and a sofa, everything white or black, a wet bar, a big TV, CD player. Buddy moves into the doorway, peers inside.

Kenneth is trying to find a radio station while Maurice and White Boy Bob ransack the place. White Boy Bob checks under the mattress.

WHITE BOY BOB

Hey –

Maurice and Kenneth look over expectantly.

I found a rubber.

MAURICE

White Boy, the man's not gonna hide no diamonds under the fuckin' mattress.

Maurice looks out the door, sees Buddy in the doorway.

Where's Foley?

BUDDY

Checkin' the other rooms, like you said.

MAURICE

(*to White Boy*)

Go keep an eye on him.

White Boy Bob slips out of the room. Maurice turns to Kenneth, who's still playing with the stereo.

Kenneth, fuck the radio, put on a CD.

KENNETH

(*looking them over*)

I don't recognize none of these bands.

MAURICE

Just pick one, put it on.

INT. HALLWAY (UPSTAIRS). NIGHT

White Boy Bob watches from the end of the hall as Foley peers into each of the bedrooms. Foley sees a back staircase and starts down. A moment later, White Boy Bob follows.

INT. HALLWAY (DOWNSTAIRS). NIGHT

White Boy Bob comes down the stairs. No sign of Foley. White Boy starts down one hallway, then turns back. Now he's lost. He opens a door, starts to walk into a closet, then backs out. He goes down the hall, turns into . . .

INT. KITCHEN. NIGHT

White Boy Bob enters, calls out tentatively.

WHITE BOY BOB

Uh, Foley?

He takes in the huge room, the massive sub-zero refrigerator. He moves to the freezer, opens it, takes in the frozen steaks.

Cool.

INT. HALLWAY (DOWNSTAIRS). NIGHT

Foley quietly moves to the doorway, peers into the kitchen, watches as White Boy Bob starts going through the freezer, taking out steaks and stacking them up on the counter. Foley shakes his head and moves on.

INT. LIBRARY (DOWNSTAIRS). NIGHT

Dark. As Foley steps into the doorway, we boom down to reveal a lighted aquarium in foreground. He comes into the room, sits down in an armchair beside the fish tank.

He leans close to the glass, stares at the fish a moment. He sees a door reflected there and turns to look across the room, sees how the phone cord disappears underneath.

FOLEY

They cut the lines, Richard.

Silence. The door opens and we see a terrified Richard Ripley sitting on top of a toilet, the phone in his lap.

RIPLEY

Foley? That you?

FOLEY

How are you, Richard?

RIPLEY

Jesus Christ, what the hell are you doing here? What's going on? Who's upstairs?

FOLEY

Maurice Miller, couple of his friends.

RIPLEY

Maurice? From Lompoc? Good God.

Ripley moves to the doorway.

Have they got Midge up there?

FOLEY

What kinda man lets a woman answer the door, this time a night?

RIPLEY

We thought it might be her husband. Sometimes he comes and checks up on her. She told him I was down in Florida.

FOLEY

A minute or two, you're gonna wish you were.

Ripley looks at him. Foley pats the back of a chair.

Why don't you come on over here, sit down, Richard, have a look at your fish.

EXT. BLOOMFIELD HILLS. ROAD. NIGHT

Karen slowly negotiates her way through the snowstorm.

INT. BEDROOM. NIGHT

The music on loud (Herb Alpert – 'Tijuana Taxi'). Buddy stands in the doorway, watches Maurice, out of his coveralls, as he takes suits and sport coats from the walk-in closet to look them over. He tries on a coat, turns to the maid.

MAURICE

How do I look, mama?

MAID

Like a fag.

Maurice smiles at her, goes back into the closet. Kenneth stares at the maid, nodding slowly.

KENNETH

I think she like to tussle with me. Get boned a way she gonna remember.

She looks to the doorway, where Buddy now starts to take a step into the room, when Maurice comes out of the closet . . .

MAURICE

(*off-screen*)

Motherfucker!

He sticks his head out of the closet.

I found the safe.

Buddy backs out of the room.

EXT. RIPLEY'S HOUSE. NIGHT

Karen drives slowly past the house. White Boy Bob emerges with an armload of steaks and sets them on the front steps.

MAURICE
(*off-screen*)
White Boy! Get your ass up here!

White Boy Bob hurries back into the house.

INT. LIBRARY. NIGHT

Ripley sits on the couch across from Foley. He keeps looking up at the ceiling.

RIPLEY
What do you want from me, Jack? Name it. You want money?

FOLEY
You gonna write me a cheque?

RIPLEY
We'll go to my bank. I'll make a withdrawal.

Foley just looks at him. Buddy sticks his head in the room.

BUDDY
They found the safe.

FOLEY
You remember Buddy, don't you, Richard?

BUDDY
Yeah, hi. Nice house.

RIPLEY
Thank you.

INT. BEDROOM. CLOSET DOORWAY. NIGHT

White Boy Bob comes in as Kenneth and Maurice are getting ready to blast the safe with the shotgun and pistol.

MAURICE

We gonna open up this fucker . . .

Maurice and his boys open fire on the safe. The maid covers up as bullets begin ricocheting all over the room.

Jesus . . .!

EXT. HOUSE. NIGHT

Karen sees the muzzle flashes in the upstairs window and quickly gets out of the car.

INT. LIBRARY. NIGHT

Buddy and Ripley look up.

RIPLEY

(*gets up*)

Good God . . . they're shooting Midge!

FOLEY

(*pushes him down*)

Siddown, Dick. They're trying to open the safe, not your maid.

INT. BEDROOM. NIGHT

Maurice, Kenneth and White Boy Bob get ready to fire again.

MAURICE

A'ight, this time we gotta get the motherfuckin' *trajectory* right . . .

(*pause*)

OK, on three: one . . . two . . .

MAID

The combination is three–ten–forty-four.

They all turn to look at her, guns still pointing at the safe.

Richard's birthday.

EXT. HOUSE. NIGHT

Karen cautiously makes her way towards the front door.

INT. BEDROOM. NIGHT

Maurice finally gets the safe open. They all anxiously peer inside. Maurice narrows his eyes, reaches in, pulls out one of three toupees. He stares at it.

MAURICE

. . . the fuck is this . . .

WHITE BOY BOB

Are they dead?

He looks at White Boy Bob.

MAURICE

Go find Foley. NOW!

INT. LIBRARY. NIGHT

Foley leans forward in the chair now.

RIPLEY

I can't believe you're still angry with me, Jack, after all this time.

FOLEY

I'm not angry, Richard.

(*staring at the tank*)

In fact, I'm completely relaxed. Thing is, I can't tell if it's the fish that're cooling me out or all those uncut diamonds on the bottom of the tank there.

Ripley sags, closes his eyes.

BUDDY

Damn –

And now Buddy takes a closer look and now we, too, see that, strewn about the bottom of the aquarium, are dozens of uncut diamonds of various sizes.

FOLEY

Dumbfuck Glenn was right, there's about five million worth in there, wouldn't you say, Richard?

RIPLEY

Five point two.

BUDDY

They look like plain old rocks.

FOLEY

They sure do.

He gets up, looks at Buddy.

Go get a bag.

Foley turns to Richard as Buddy comes back into the room with a plastic bag, starts reaching into the tank.

I were you, I'd get up and run.

RIPLEY

I'm not leaving Midge.

FOLEY

Don't be an asshole, Richard. They're gonna kill you.

RIPLEY

If that's my fate, so be it. I'm not leaving.

(*pause*)

I love her, Jack.

Foley looks at Buddy. Now what?

BUDDY

C'mon.

Foley just looks at Ripley, who doesn't move.

FOLEY

Good luck, Richard.

MAURICE

(*off-screen*)

Someone down here?

Buddy and Foley slip out the other door, down the hall, just as Maurice walks in, some of Ripley's clothes over his arm.

Well, if it isn't the Ripper hisself.

RIPLEY

Are those *my* suits?

MAURICE

Where you been hiding, Dick?

EXT. HOUSE. NIGHT

A now-freezing Karen hugs a retaining wall, watches as Foley and Buddy emerge from the house.

At the van Buddy leans under the dash. Foley looks up at the house, where we see shadows moving about in the upstairs window, hear the faint pumping of the music. We hear the van start.

BUDDY

OK.

Buddy straightens up, looks at Foley.

Come *on.*

FOLEY

Shit.

BUDDY

What?

FOLEY

They're gonna rape the maid, aren't they?

BUDDY

From the looks of those boys, the Ripper too.

FOLEY

And then they'll kill 'em.

BUDDY

At least.

Foley looks at the diamonds in the bag.

FOLEY

We made it, didn't we?

BUDDY

All you gotta do is get in.

Again Foley looks at the diamonds, then . . .

FOLEY

I'm going back inside.

BUDDY

I'll go with you.

Foley finally hands him the bag with the diamonds in it.

FOLEY

No, you dump the van, meet me at the airport. I'll take one of Ripley's cars.

BUDDY

Jack –

FOLEY

Listen, Buddy, the shit that's about to go down, you'll be on the phone with your sister for a month. Let me do this part alone.

Buddy just looks at him.

I'm saying this isn't your problem. Far as I'm concerned, we're square.

Foley turns to go.

BUDDY

Hey . . .

Buddy hands him his gun. Foley takes it, stuffs it in the back of his pants, and then turns back to the house.

FOLEY

Now get outta here.

Focus on Karen as she watches Foley go back inside. A moment later, the van pulls out of the driveway. Karen makes a decision, starts for the side of the house.

INT. RIPLEY'S HOUSE. THE FOYER. NIGHT

Foley enters and we hear the maid scream. Foley starts up the stairs.

INT. LIBRARY. NIGHT

Maurice and White Boy Bob both have their guns to Ripley's head.

RIPLEY

(*hears the scream*)

Midge –

MAURICE

Forget about her. Tell me where the money's at.

RIPLEY

Foley's got it.

MAURICE

Where the fuck is Foley?

INT. HALLWAY (UPSTAIRS). NIGHT

Foley comes up the stairs, heads for Ripley's bedroom. The door is closed now.

FOLEY

Midge?

He steps to one side, is about to reach for the knob, when suddenly the door is blasted off its hinges.

INT. KITCHEN (DOWNSTAIRS). NIGHT

Karen comes through the door, hears the gunshot, stops cold.

INT. HALLWAY (UPSTAIRS). NIGHT

Foley steps into the doorway and we see Kenneth and the maid bare, both sitting up in bed, Kenneth racking the shotgun, the maid turning away from him, gathering the covers that hang off her side of the bed . . .

. . . and coming around to throw them like a net at Kenneth as the shotgun goes off and the covers catch fire as Foley pumps one-two-three shots into Kenneth somewhere under there.

INT. LIBRARY. NIGHT

Ripley tries to get away.

RIPLEY

Midge!

Maurice grabs him by the collar, spins him around and whips him across the face with his gun. He and White Boy Bob then both hit Ripley on the head until he goes down and stays down.

MAURICE

(*to White Boy Bob*)

You take the front stairs, I'll take the back.

INT. BEDROOM. NIGHT

The maid jumps up and drags the burning covers from the bed and sees Kenneth now, the bullet holes in his chest, and stares blankly back at him. She then looks at Foley.

MAID
(*cold*)

Where's Dick?

FOLEY

Downstairs.

(*pause*)

But wait here. There's two more.

INT. HALLWAY (UPSTAIRS). NIGHT

Foley starts out of the room and immediately hears . . .

WHITE BOY BOB

Hold it, asshole!

Foley sees White Boy Bob at the bottom of the stairs.

Drop the gun.

Nowhere to go, Foley has to comply.

Now stay right there. Don't move.

White Boy Bob starts to jog up the stairs two at a time, all the while keeping his eyes fixed on Foley.

Maurice! I got Foley!

INT. BACK STAIRCASE. NIGHT

Maurice starts up the back stairs.

WHITE BOY BOB

Maurice! Up here!

A moment later, Karen comes out of the kitchen into the downstairs hallway – just missing Maurice.

INT. STAIRCASE. NIGHT

White Boy Bob gets maybe half-way up when he catches a toe on one of the risers and pitches forward. Stupidly, he tries to break his fall with the elbow of his gun hand and ends up jamming his chin down on to the muzzle of his gun, which, unfortunately for him, goes off, firing a bullet through his head and killing him instantly.

To say the least, Foley is stunned by this freak accident. He stands there looking at the dead bulk on the stairs.

FOLEY
(*finally*)
You learn from doing.

Foley bends down to pick up his gun and we see Maurice coming up the back staircase, his gun raised and now firing away.

Foley is forced to jump back behind a pillar as Maurice keeps firing at him, shots ricocheting off the pillar, the railing, the wall . . .

INT. HALLWAY (DOWNSTAIRS). NIGHT

Karen hugs the wall at the sound of the gunshots, sees Ripley lying on the floor of the study.

INT. HALLWAY (UPSTAIRS). NIGHT

We hear click as the breech opens on Maurice's now empty .45. Foley steps out from behind the pillar and calmly bends down, picks up his gun. Maurice still walking forward . . .

MAURICE
Jack, you don't use a gun, do you?

FOLEY
Not until recently.

MAURICE
(*still coming*)
Nervous?

FOLEY

A little.

MAURICE

(*getting close*)

This kind of set-up, you don't have any idea what the fuck you're doing – do you?

FOLEY

You're right. So why take a chance –

Foley pulls the trigger. Click. Maurice hesitates, surprised that Foley would pull the trigger, then the two of them at the same time rush each other, begin a messy mano a mano, *now using their spent guns as bludgeons.*

INT. LIBRARY. NIGHT

As Karen carefully comes into the room, Ripley lets out a low groan. She's bending down to check him when her phone rings.

INT. HALLWAY (UPSTAIRS). NIGHT

Foley and Maurice grapple on the floor near the head of the stairs.

INT. LIBRARY. NIGHT

Karen answers her phone and checks Ripley.

KAREN

Hello?

CRUZ

(*phone*)

We're a few minutes away. Just sit tight, stay outta the house till we get there, understand?

KAREN

O-K . . .

INT. HALLWAY (UPSTAIRS). NIGHT

Foley finally shoves Maurice down the stairs. Maurice rolls down a few steps, right over White Boy Bob, as Foley gets up, runs back to the bedroom.

INT. BEDROOM. NIGHT

Foley enters, goes straight to Kenneth's body, begins searching for the shotgun (*lifting the covers, turning over the body, etc.*) *with no success.*

FOLEY

Shit . . .

INT. STAIRWELL. NIGHT

As Maurice attempts to prise the gun out from under the dead bulk of White Boy Bob.

INT. BEDROOM. NIGHT

Foley, exasperated, stands back up.

MIDGE
(*off-screen*)

This what you want?

Foley looks to where Midge stands – now back in her bathrobe, but, more importantly, clutching the shotgun. Foley crosses and takes it from her, begins to stride out of the room, when –

It's empty.

Foley just looks at her.

INT. STAIRWELL. NIGHT

Maurice finally rolls White Boy Bob over, grabs the gun.

INT. BEDROOM. NIGHT

Foley sticks his hand in Kenneth's coveralls, comes out with a shell, loads the gun, snaps it shut.

INT. STAIRWELL. NIGHT

Maurice cocks the pistol, takes a step up the stairs.

KAREN
(*off-screen*)

Maurice –

Maurice spins around, points his gun down at Karen, now standing in the foyer, her own gun pointing up at him.

EXT. RIPLEY'S HOUSE. NIGHT

Raymond Cruz and several green-and-whites arrive.

INT. BEDROOM. NIGHT

Foley, about to exit, stops cold as he hears two gunshots, then a body fall.

He stands still. Not sure who was just shot. After a long moment, we then hear:

KAREN
(*off-screen*)

Jack?

He sees Midge looking at him, closes his eyes, sags against the wall.

I know you're up there.

INT. FOYER. NIGHT

Foley steps into the hallway, his ski mask now pulled down over his face. He holds Kenneth's shotgun in one hand and his pistol in another.

KAREN

Come on, Jack – don't.

FOLEY

Pretend I'm somebody else.

KAREN

You think I'd shoot you?

Foley brings up the pistol and the shotgun. And now we hear the sirens.

FOLEY

If you don't, one of those guys will.

KAREN

What're you now, a desperado? Put the guns down.

FOLEY

I told you, I'm not going back.

He raises the guns hip-high and we hear sounds behind Karen, but she's quick to raise her hand, though she doesn't turn or look around.

KAREN

Don't do this. Please.

They stand there staring at each other.

FOLEY

No more time-outs.

He raises the guns. She sadly shakes her head.

KAREN

You win, Jack.

She fires and he falls to the staircase, dropping the guns, grabbing hold of his left thigh. And now Cruz and several other cops enter. Karen motions them to stop.

CRUZ

Karen, I told you not to –

KAREN

Wait, I know him – OK?

She goes up the staircase to where Foley is lying and gently lifts the ski mask and looks at his sad eyes.

I'm sorry, Jack, but I can't shoot you.

FOLEY

You just did, for Christ sake.

KAREN

You know what I mean.

She glances about, makes sure no one can hear, then leans closer to him.

I wish things were different. I'm sorry, Jack.

Foley looks like he's in pain. He watches as she walks back down the stairs. As a couple of uniform cops rush past her and pick up Foley, a shaky Ripley staggers into the foyer.

MIDGE

Richard!

She comes running down the stairs into his arms. They embrace. He looks at Foley over her shoulder.

RIPLEY

(*sympathetic*)

Listen, Jack . . .

(*but then*)

What'd you do with my diamonds?

Foley just looks at him.

EXT. BUSY STREET. NIGHT

Buddy pulls the van into an alley. He jumps out, jogs back to the street and hails a cab.

INT. CAB. NIGHT

Suddenly gets in, bangs on the bulletproof glass.

BUDDY

The airport.

The cab pulls away. Buddy glances up front, then pulls the Ziploc bag from his coat and holds it up. There's a bit of water in along with the diamonds. A tiny fish swims in the water. Something about this makes Buddy smile as we . . .

DISSOLVE TO:

EXT. KAREN'S HOTEL. MORNING

The sun is out. The sky is clear.

KAREN

(*voice-over*)

They don't know yet if they want to bring him up on the homicides.

INT. KAREN'S HOTEL ROOM. MORNING

Karen on the phone. Her suitcase on the bed.

KAREN

I doubt if they will. The Bureau's put a detainer on him, so when they're through with him here he'll go back to Florida.

INT. MARSHALL SISCO'S SITTING ROOM. MORNING

Marshall on the phone.

MARSHALL

You gonna go get him?

KAREN

It's possible. Why?

MARSHALL

I was just thinking . . . you could have a nice time with him on the plane – like picking up where your interlude, or whatever you call it, left off. And then throw him in the can.

KAREN

He knew what he was doing. Nobody forced him to rob banks.

MARSHALL

My little girl, the tough babe.

Karen hangs up, stares thoughtfully out the window.

INT. PRISON CELL. DAY

Where Foley stands staring out of his window.

VOICE

Foley.

As Foley turns around and faces a federal marshal in the doorway, we see that Foley's hands and feet are shackled.

INT./EXT. PRISON STATION GARAGE. DAY

The marshal leads Foley from the building to where a black government van waits. The marshal helps Foley inside.

FEDERAL MARSHAL

Have a nice trip.

(*looks off-screen*)

I'll get the other one.

INT./EXT. VAN. DAY

Foley sits down, stares at the floor. He looks depressed. We hear the front door open, then close.

KAREN

(*off-screen*)

Jack?

He looks to where Karen looks at him through a steel grate that separates the front from the back.

I got you a present, something for the road.

She pushes a Zippo through the grate.

I have to take it away, though, soon as the ride's over.

Before Foley can say anything, the back door is opened once more and the marshal helps another prisoner – a black man with a shaved head – into the back of the van.

FEDERAL MARSHAL

Jack Foley meet Hejira Henry.

An annoyed Foley stares at the guy as the marshal shuts the door, then gets in up front with Karen.

FOLEY

Hejira? What kinda name is that?

HEJIRA

Islamic.

FOLEY

What's it mean, 'No Hair'?

HEJIRA

The Hejira was the flight of Mohammed from Mecca in 622.

FOLEY

The flight?

HEJIRA

The brothers in Leavenworth gave me the name.

FOLEY

You were at Leavenworth, huh?

HEJIRA

For a time.

FOLEY

Meaning?

HEJIRA

Meaning time came, I left.

FOLEY

You busted out?

HEJIRA

I prefer to call it an exodus from an undesirable place.

FOLEY

(*interested now*)

And how long was it before they caught up with you?

HEJIRA

That time?

FOLEY

There were others.

HEJIRA

Yeah. That was the ninth.

FOLEY

(*really interested*)

The *ninth*?

HEJIRA

Ten, you count the prison hospital in Ohio I walked away from.

FOLEY

You must be some kinda walker, Henry.

HEJIRA

Hejira.

FOLEY

And so now you're off to Glades.

HEJIRA

Apparently, yeah. I was supposed to leave last night with the lady marshal, but for some reason she wanted to wait.

FOLEY

(*looks at Karen*)

She did, huh.

HEJIRA

Cheaper I guess, take us both down in one van.

FOLEY

Yeah, could be. Or maybe she thought we'd have a lot to talk about.

HEJIRA

Like what?

FOLEY

I don't know.

(*pause*)

It's a long way down to Florida.

Foley glances at her, then turns back to Hejira Henry and considers the guy; a smile on Foley's face, his spirits a little higher than when he first sat down, as we then . . .

CUT TO BLACK

Credits

CAST

JACK FOLEY	George Clooney
BANK EMPLOYEE	Jim Robinson
BANK CUSTOMER	Elgin Marlow
TELLER/LORETTA	Donna Frenzel
COP #1/BANK	Manny Suarez
COP #2/BANK	Keith Hudson
CHINO	Luis Guzman
LULU	Paul Soileau
PUP	Scott Allen
ADELE	Catherine Keener
BUDDY BRAGG	Ving Rhames
PARKING LOT WOMAN	Susan Hatfield
KAREN SISCO	Jennifer Lopez
MARSHALL SISCO	Dennis Farina
GLENN MICHAELS	Steve Zahn
MAURICE MILLER	Don Cheadle
WHITE BOXER	Brad Martin
RICHARD RIPLEY	Albert Brooks
HIMEY	James Black
DANIEL BURDON/FBI	Wendell B. Harris Jr.
LIBRARY GUARD	Chuck Castleberry
FOURTH FBI MAN	Chic Daniel
OLD ELEVATOR LADY	Connie Sawyer
OLD ELEVATOR GENT	Phil Perlman
WHITE BOY BOB	Keith Loneker
KENNETH	Isaiah Washington
RAYMOND CRUZ	Paul Calderon
OFFICER GRANT	Gregory H. Alpert
MOSELLE	Viola Davis
RIPLEY PRSONNEL	Mark Brown
RECEPTIONIST	Sandra Ives
RIPLEY GUARD	Joe Hess

WAITRESS/CELESTE	Betsy Monroe
EXECUTIVE GUY/PHILIP	Wayne Pere
EXECUTIVE GUY/ANDY	Joe Chrest
EXECUTIVE GUY #3	Joe Coyle
MIDGE	Nancy Allen
FEDERAL MARSHAL	Stephen M. Horn
STUNT COORDINATOR	G. A. Aguilar

STUNT PLAYERS

Bob Apisa	Dan Maldonado
Bruce Barbour	Steve Martinez
Jill Brown	Benny Moore
Richard Brown	Jim Palmer
Carl Ciarfalio	Eddie Perez
Douglas Crosby	Richard Piemonte
Malcolm Ian Cross	Steve Pope
Ousaun Elam	Victor Prince
Peter Epstein	Tom Rosales
Eddie Fernandez	Hash Shaalan
Romiro Gonzales	Garfield Wedderburn
Dick Hancock	Brian Williams
Chuck Jeffries	Gene Williams

CREDITS

Directed by	Steven Soderbergh
Screenplay by	Scott Frank
Produced by	Danny DeVito, Michael Shamberg Stacey Sher
Executive Producers	Barry Sonnenfeld John Hardy
Based on the Novel by	Elmore Leonard
Camera	Elliot Davis
Production Designed by	Gary Frutkoff
Editor	Anne V. Coates A.C.E.
Music by	Cliff Martinez
Music Supervisor	Anita Camarata

Costume Design	Betsy Heimann
Casting	Francine Maisler C.S.A.
Unit Production Manager	Fred Brost
First Assistant Director	Gregory Jacobs
Second Assistant Director	Trey Batchelor
Art Director	Phil Messina
Set Director	Maggie Martin
Camera Operator	Gary Jay
'A' Camera First Assistant	Duane Manwiller
'B' Camera First Assistant	Bobby Brown
Production Sound Mixer	Paul Ledford C.A.S.
Boom Operator	Keenan Wyatt
Production Office Coordinator	Lisa Becker
Production Account	Karen Eisenstadt
Script Supervisor	Wilma Garscadden-Gahret
Set Designers	Lauren Cory Keith P. Cunningham Mary Finn
Property Master	Emily Ferry
Assistant Property Master	Joy Taylor
Second Assistant Property Master	Otniel Gonzalez
Props	Brett Gollin
Stand By Painter	Chuck Eskridge
Art Department Coordinator	Blair Huizingh
Art Department Assistant	Andrea Brody
Buyer	Maike Both
Leadman	David C. Potter
Second Leadman	Jon Bush
Set Dressers	Tristan P. Bourne Harry Frierson James E. Hurd Jr. Alexander Kirst Chris Patterson
On Set Dresser	Mike Malone
Floor Covering	Shane. L. Ashton
Drapery	David Gordon
'A' Camera Second Assistant	Rodney Sandoval
'B' Camera Second Assistants	James Apted, Crispin May

Camera Operator/Steadicam	Stephen Collins
Camera Loaders	Dave Berryman, Marvin Lee
Utility Sound	Mark C. Grech, Sam Sarkar
Gaffer	Dwight D. Campbell
Best Boy Electric	Ms Simone Perusse
Electricians	Michael Lyon, Niles McElroy, John Nadeau, Gustavo Oliva, Robert Oliva, Michael Tolochko
Stage Rigging Gaffer	Charlie McIntyre
Stage Rigging Best Boy	Willie J. Gray
Location Rigging Gaffer	Dennis Lootens
Location Rigging Best Boy	Branch Marie Brunson
Key Grip	Richard Mall
Best Boy Grip	Thomas Crawford
Dolly Grip	Dave Pearlberg
Grips	Gregory Fausak, Philip Ho, David Jensen, John Seravic, Skyler Tegland
Rigging Key Grip	Renton Medcalf
Rigging Best Boy Grip	Mike McGuire
Special Effects by	Lynn-Wenger Productions Inc. Carol Lynn Wenger Clifford P. Wenger
Special Effects Key	Eric Roberts
Special Effects	Ryan Arndt, Craig Barnett Derrick Crane, Don Hastings, Scott Hastings, Darrell Roberts, Mike J. Sasgen, Larry M. Shorts
Motion Effects	Don Gray
Costume Supervisor	Nick Scarano
Key Costumer	Joyce Kogut
Key Set Costumers	Brian Callahan, Lori Stilson
Costumers	Darryl Athons Jorge J. Gonzales
Assistant to Ms Heimann	Sabrina A. Rosen
Cutter/Fitter	Leslie Miller
Key Makeup Artist	Kathrine James
Assistant Makeup Artist	Bill Corso
Jennifer Lopez's Makeup Artist	Margot Boccia

Ving Rhames' Makeup Artist	Anita Gibson
Key Hairstylist	Bonnie Clevering
Assistant Hairstylist	Deborah Mills
Hairstylist for George Clooney	Waldo Sanchez
Location Managers	Gregory H. Alpert Kenneth D. Lavet
First Assistant Accountant	Monica Muehlhause-Horn
Second Assistant Accountant	Marybeth Martin-Eck
Payroll Accountants	Cathy Marshall Tomothy P. Tundel
Construction Accountant	Cynthia Vandenbulcke
Assistant Production Coordinators	Brian Ted Deiker, Dale Becker, Channing Work
Production Secretary	Denis Hennelly
Production Office Assistants	Christopher Jerome Brown Cindy Glass, Bach Nguyen
Production Office Intern	Jeff White
2nd 2nd Assistant Director	Michael Risoli
Additional 2nd Assistant Director	David Bernstein
Casting Director's Associates	Kathryn Eisenstein Jon Scott Strotheide
Extras Casting	Axium Casting, Rich King
Unit Publicist	Spooky Stevens
Still Photographer	Merrick Morton
Assistant to Mr Soderbergh and Mr Hardy	Caitlin Maloney
Assistant to Mr DeVito	Pam Abdy
Assistant to Mr Shamberg	Wes Clark
Assistant to Ms Sher	Jennifer Kuczaj
Assistant to Mr Frank	Laura Stover
Research Assistant to Mr Leonard	Greg Sutter
Assistant to Mr Clooney	Amy Minda Cohen
Assistant to Ms Lopez	Arlene Rodriguez
Assistant to Mr Rhames	Christopher J. Ford
Set Production Assistants	Tammy Dickson, Buz Presock
DGA Trainee	Staci Lamkin

Stand-ins	Joe Coyle, Christina Parsa, Garfield Wedderburn
Construction Coordinator	Chris Snyder
General Foreman	Gary Gagliardo
Location Foreman	William Gideon
Office Foreman/Purchaser	John Moore
Propmaker Mill Foreman	Gerry Forrest
Propmaker Welding Foreman	Bud Kucia
Propmaker Foreman	Devlin Lerew
Toolman/Propmaker Foreman	Jim Paniagua
Labour Foremen	Theodise Belli, Louie Esparza, Anthony J. Saenz, Tony Salazar
Paint Supervisor	Hank Giardina
Paint Foreman	James Seegar
Location Paint Foreman	Steven J. Kerlagon
Painter 2nd	Mark Woodworth
Plasterer Supervisor	Walter R. Buckallew
Plaster Foremen	Shane Buckallew, Robert Montano
Transportation Coordinator	James C. Taylor
Transportation Captains	David Jernigan, Fred Wilson
Set Captain	Richard Chouinard
Picture Car Captain	Myron Shepherd
Driver/Generator Operator's	Cal Masoner Clinton J. Taylor Henry Travers
Mechanic	Donald Harback

DRIVERS

Lester Carlstein	Horst Harter
Brian Delahanty	Lou Leucart
Ronald Demond	Bill Purviance
Billy Esparza	Danny Routhicaux
Allan Falco	Craig Scott
Jill Falco	Ed Shekter
Bill Gray	Phil Strauss
David Goodman	Jacqueline Travers
Bob Hargraves	Launi Varbel

Transport Office Assistant	Margaret M. Wilson
First Aid	Gordon Aaron Greer
	Linda Leinwohl
	Forrest L. Painter
Technical Advisor	Reel Deal Technical Advisors
	Chic Daniel
Catering	Entertainment Catering
	Eric Vignando
Cook	Clement Bacque
Catering Assistants	Jose Plasencia
	Victor Solorzano
Craft Service	Charles, J. Adams,
	Richard Cody, Buz Kramer,
	Noel B. Harris, Timothy Worley
Supervising Sound Editor	Larry Blake
Re-Recording Mixer	Larry Blake, Gerry Lentz
Post Production Supervisor	Caitlin Maloney
First Assistant Editor	Robb Sullivan
Second Assistant Editor	John Axelrad
Assistant Editor	Brad Dean
All-Purpose Sound Editor	Aaron Glascock
Dialog Editors	Michael Chock
	Marvin Walowitz
Foley Editors	Ezra Dweck, John Dunn
Assistant Sound Editor	Oscar Mitt
Post Production Sound Services	Weddington Productions
Foley by	Alicia Stevenson, Dawn Fintor,
	Paul Stevenson
Foley Mixer	David Betancourt
Foley Recordist	Carrie Cashman
Foley Recorded at	Twentieth Century Fox
ADR Group	L. A. Maddogs
Re-Recorded at	Soundelux Vine Street Studios
Soundelux Recordist	Eric Flickinger

MUSIC CREW

Programming	Tim Goldsworthy
Keyboards	Darren Morris

Guitar/Bass/Engineering	Phil Mossman
Engineer	Tom Fritze
Score Recorded at	The Studio
Music Consultant	Amanda Demme
Music Coordinator	Kaylin Frank
Assistant to Ms Camarata	Cari Cohen
Digital Visual Effects by	Cinesite Inc.
VFX Supervisor	Brad Kuehn
VFX Associate Producer	Chris Del Conte
Digital Compositor	Sean Mackenzie
Digital Compositor	Will McCoy
CGI Animator	Allen Ruilova
Roto Supervisor	Karen Klein
Digital Artist	Erin M. Gullen
Digital Artist	Gilbert Gonzales
Digital Coordinator	Kimberly Spear
VFX Assistant Editor	Jason Sullivan
Post Production Accountant	Leah Holmes
Post Production Assistant	David Conley
Titles & Opticals	Howard Anderson
Negative Cutter	Gary Burritt
Colour Timer	Mike Milliken

FLORIDA CREW

Production Supervisor	Mary Morgan
Assistant Props	Charles P. Guanli Jr.
Utility Sound	Jerry Rose
Assistant Location Manager	Lori Byers
Accounting Assistant	Lisa Etherington

LOUISIANA CREW

Camera Operator	Francis James
Utility Sound	Jimmy Armstrong

MICHIGAN CREW

Production Supervisor	Pat Chapman
Utility Sound	Gail Carroll-Coe
Assistant Location Manager	Thomas M. Jacob

Locations Assistant	James Maxwell
Accountant	Jean N. Kalanzi
Snow Maker	Dieter Sturm

'Spanish Grease'
Written by William Correa and Melvin Lastie
Performed By Willie Bobo
Courtesy of Verve Records
By arrangement with PolyGram Film & TV Music

'Brown and Blue'
Written by David Troncoso
Performed by Pancho Sanchez
Courtesy of Concord Records

'Watermelon Man'
Written by Herbie Hancock
Performed by Pancho Sanchez
Courtesy of Concord Records

'Let Me Call You Sweetheart'
Written by Leo Friedman and Beth Slater Whitson
Arranged and Performed by (Piano Player)

'Fight the Power (Part 2)'
Written by Chris Jasper, Marvin Isley, Ronald Isley,
O'Kelly Isley, Ernest Isley, Rudolph Isley
Performed by The Isley Brothers
Courtesy of T-Neck Records
By arrangement with Sony Music Licensing

'Canadian Sunset'
Written by Eddie Haywood and Norman Gimbal
Performed by Esquivel
Courtesy of Reprise Records
By arrangement with Warner Special Products

'One Note Samba'
Written by Antonio Carlos Jobim
Performed by Walter Wanderly
Courtesy of G.N.P. Crescendo Records

'Girl From Ipanema'
Written by Antonio Carlos Jobim
Performed by Walter Wanderly
Courtesy of G.N.P. Crescendo Records

'It's Your Thing'
Written by Ronald Isley, O'Kelly Isley
and Rudolph Isley
Performed by The Isley Brothers
Courtesy of T-Neck Records
By arrangement with Sony Music Licensing

'Flosso Bosso'
Written and Performed by Harry Garfield